Enigmatic Years

By Naila Abdulla Ph.D

First edition published May 2021

All production design are trademarks.
For information regarding bulk purchases of this book, digital purchase and special discounts, please contact the author.

ISBN Print: 978-1-7775430-0-6

ISBN Ebook: 978-1-7775430-2-0

Contents

Acknowledgements

The writing of this book is purely circumstantial as the COVID-19 pandemic provided the time and impetus to make it a reality. First and foremost, my deep and heartfelt gratitude for the gift of education to His Highness Prince Karim Aga Khan. As a Muslim female to be equipped with quality education during the '50's and '60's helped lay the foundation for continued attainment of higher education and my ability to cope with several challenging situations.

I attribute a significantly improved text to Nazim Karim for his meticulous and diligent editing. His characteristic cheerfulness, patience and stretching beyond the role of editing to engaging in its content with useful comments and suggestions and providing the impetus to bring this book to fruition. I am profoundly grateful for his unfaltering interest and far surpassing the call of editing.

I am grateful to Dr. Shiraz Kurji for his moral support and positive comments providing the inspiration to not only complete the book but write its epilogue. I recognize that despite other demands on his time, he promptly responded with suggestions for improvement.

A number of friends and colleagues provided valuable goodwill, interest and support to the successful completion of this book. I acknowledge Nashir Pirani for his creativity in the art for the cover and his enthusiasm in meeting its critical path despite incessant revisions to which I kept subjecting it. My deep appreciation to colleagues Firoz Rhemtulla, Dr. Esmail Merani, Nasim Teja, and Yasmin Dossa for their contributions in writing articles or providing snapshots to lend this book its inclusive read. I acknowledge the support for marketing and publishing ideas provided by Mehboob Daya and Nazir Alibhai.

The incidents and anecdotes presented are depicted as my memory best recollects them. It has not been my intention to embarrass anyone but to represent past accounts of events shared with my classmates and friends. My apologies to anyone who may take umbrage at anything within these accounts.

Finally, I'd like to thank the general reader for their interest. Please be assured that the core of this book lies in the voice drawing your attention to teenage years, recollecting fond memories, and fresh recollections of the happy and carefree years and lessons learnt through life experiences

Happy Reading!

My Dear Munira.

A series of deftly comic narratives for a feel-good read.

I hope you enjoy this short & simple read.

Truly appreciate your friendship & caring.

Much love

Naila

Paint Your Life
by tree.cards

Life is like a piece of art,
It requires lots of heart.
Choose your paint and your brush,
Take your time, avoid the rush.
Before you paint, choose your theme,
Don't be afraid to follow your dream.
It's alright to make a mistake.
Your painting is real, not fake.
Look at your painting, don't be crying,
Begin again, keep on trying.
Your painting is never fully complete,
Enjoy the process, make sure it's sweet.

Introduction

It's hard to imagine an academic home to teenagers who were arguably vaguely aware of the world around them. It was an era of limited telephone and television access and communication was certainly not what it is today. The diverse cluster of students was either shy, demure, boisterous, disruptive, brilliant, intelligent, average performer, bully, rich, poor, confident or timid. Each individual was exploring, searching, and dealing with issues typical of any teenager.

This academic home is Aga Khan High School Nairobi, established in 1961 in the suburb of Westlands during the colonial period, which ended in 1963. This location was zoned as a residential neighborhood of Nairobi, which developed over the past 60 years as an affluent area for businesses and residences, and now has an official address located on Waiyaki Way, seven kilometres north-west of Nairobi city centre.

As alumnae of the school, especially the girls, we recognize ourselves as privileged and owe deep gratitude to its founder, His Highness Prince Karim Aga Khan, a remarkable man known for his foresight, generosity, imagination, and wisdom. He allowed us the gift of education, which in turn allowed us and our children to Ivy League and other respected universities globally. He has been the inspiring founder of schools, colleges, and universities for recognizing education to be a democratic pillar.

Enigmatic Years, has focused on an assemblage of the author's perspectives and disciplines from our teenage years at Aga Khan High School, Nairobi. To skillfully compile teenage experiences has been a need to relive those years re-exploring the fun shared, lessons learnt, and development based on a strong educational foundation.

Schoolmates, classmates, and other baby boomers especially from East Africa may enjoy this read with flashbacks to the intriguing and unforgettable moments of our formative years, elated, blissful, happy, and enigmatic because how we would fare was unpredictable. Baby boomers who lived in East Africa during the '60s may enjoy this relaxing read and relate to the stories, as many would have lived through similar experiences in their schools at that time.

We hope the younger audiences reading this book get a glimpse of the fun-packed life their parents and grandparents enjoyed but their transformation into adults bore responsibilities. The lesson to be learnt from one's teenage years is that the energy and vitality, not unique to us, has belonged to every generation, making it essential to balancing these precious years with a healthy ethos for academics and play, so as to meet the challenges of life - with positive attitudes and outcomes.

These years slip through the passage of time to be embedded in the recesses of our minds, being recalled upon demand. Capturing and detailing our past as "Enigmatic Years" seems appropriate, for even without realizing the importance of this period's trampoline effect on our life long achievements has been inexplicable, bewildering, and perplexing. Compared to the world today, our secluded and sheltered environment allowed us to revel in our own naiveté. Our teenage years were safer, free of the internet and Social Media, and generally untouched by extreme materialism influencing our thinking, behaviour, and actions.

Recollections of our magical High School experiences brings a voice to our shared experiences and treasured moments. Little did we realize that our simple ways, carefree days, and playful times were to disappear as we first left Kenya to study abroad and then to live in Europe, Canada, the United States, and the Middle East. Fortunately, our sensibilities, bonding, and friendships have remained strong to overcome geographical distances, decades of separation, and responsibilities, to capture the legacy of our early years. Aided by technology, our persistent efforts at locating past friends for renewed connections, reunions, and conversations, have bridged time gaps, as if they were short and recent. Memories are treasure houses capable of instantaneous mirth, smiles, and reflections in tough times, adulthood, and our golden years of life. Often, one's recollections of a shared moment may be - different but the ability to laugh and share the moment can be gratifying. To provide a balanced read, classmates were invited to co-author chapters and collaborate in their impressions of high school years for varied opinions and perspectives for an all-inclusive recollection not confined only to the author.

Having lived our childhood during disciplined times, we never imagined our parents could have been young, full of vitality and vigour. I am sure our children formulate similar opinions about their parents, and many times find us boring, unable to chill or be 'cool' but that is the cycle of life and we must find inner grace to understand and accept their limited world view. We seem to have maintained a semblance of balance through life and I reflect on Albert Einstein comparing life to riding a bicycle and keeping balance through moving.

During our teenage years, we coped with physical and emotional changes, with little parental guidance. Other than school and homework, life consisted of meeting friends occasionally, rare trips to coffee shops in town on Saturdays when one had money, going to our Jamatkhana every evening, visiting and entertaining relatives, neighbours, and our parent's friends. Much time was spent with parents, their friends, and other elders.

At a time of limited resources and colonial oppression, our parents made great sacrifices in educating us and being a constant source of encouragement even though we seldom were the centre of attention, as children are today. Our lives were not boring as we never stopped adventuring, embracing the inner child, staying fearless and positive. Being brought up in the colonial era, we were products of Western civilization, spoke English, listened to music, wore European clothes, and were subsumed in European culture without realizing history's impact on the development of our personas.

As we scattered for Universities and Colleges globally, friendships between both genders remained strong. Our high school girl-friend circle shared secrets and confidences, and we were perhaps accused of being cliquish, but were not aware of being so. We shared a simple mid-morning snack of salted boiled corn, for 5 cents, a couple of times a week and found humour in most situations.

Our parents unanimously considered us their angels, incapable of mischief. Contrarily, this book recounts tales of adventures and misadventures never discovered by them. Our pranks involved hitch-hiking, spying on teachers, helping a teacher elope, blackmailing, stealing coconut candies, reducing tire pressure in luxury cars after Jamatkhana services, forging forms for travel and creating problems whilst travelling, to endless episodes of harassing boys who fancied girls in our circle, girls' boycotting physics tests, our preference for sitting and chatting, as opposed to running cross-country track, to walking our residential areas during school holidays.

Post-independence, Asians lived through challenging times, with minorities being targeted. However, we were hardly aware of reverse discrimination, hardships, and difficulties. My maternal grandmothers were "Jangbaris" originating from the Persian Gulf Region of Iran or from Gujarat in western India. Life was normal with our grandmothers, mixing Kutchi, Swahili and English in their soft-spoken conversations, influenced by coastal Kiswahili, poetic prose, lyrical qualities layered with rhythm. As an example, one might hear this sentence in a casual conversation:

Munjo dil me dhadke kama electric pankho," translated as "My heart beats like an electric fan." The sentence is a mix of Kutchi, Swahili and English.

We as teenagers simplified our greetings to:

Hi, Ki Ai (Kutchi) or Hi, Kemche (Gujrati) or Hi, how are you?

Trips with friends in the '60s were not encouraged, permissible or remotely entertained. Persuading our parents to allow travel trips was a herculean task but gained approval based on parent consultations, discussions with other parents, and collective nagging pressure from us. The current hands-on style of parenting was totally contrary to our growing experience in the '60s and surviving teenage-hood was a miracle. Seatbelts and travel "safety" were unknown to us as we accepted any mode of transportation if it got us to where we wished to travel. Although parents consulted with other parents, we should never have been granted permission for many outings as we were immature and incapable of sound decisions in case of hazards. Fortunately, we enjoyed our fun times and survived our teenage years into adulthood.

The Aga Khan's vision of an educated person is one who can reinforce the foundations of identity in a way that reinvigorates it and strengthens one to withstand the stresses

15

from things outside our control. There is a moral obligation and a price tag to receiving education and using achievement to benefit humanity. It is like currency needing to be spent selflessly, as self-satisfaction and personal aggrandizement for oneself is akin to hoarding the blessings that we have been fortunate to receive.

Accomplishments from the batch at Aga Khan High School Nairobi include a sea of widespread achievements, with some stellar performers in academia and administration. School and classmates have remarkable contributions in their field of endeavour benefitting their industry and country enjoying great achievements similar to Esmail's narrative later in this book. It is gratifying that some, despite earning highly-recognized accreditations, have used their hard work and talent to be humanists with global contributions and have opted to selflessly volunteer their lives to helping the marginalized. It is humbling to identify our High school performers like Professor Azim Nanji, now on the Board of Directors of Global Centre for Pluralism; Professor Ali Asani, lecturer at Harvard; Iqbal Paroo, former CEO, President and Chancellor of Hahnemann University International Health Care Executive; and Firoz Rasul, President of the Aga Khan University.

Our reunions met with a recounting of stories, non-stop laughter and unanimous acquiescence at our migration successes. The exchange of reflections has been engaging as classmates relate to the stories irrespective of listeners not having been active participants in the incident related. Reunions allowed the luxury of going back in time to our carefree days, enjoying the anecdotes, laughing at our innocent naivety and fast-forwarding to the individuals we have become.

School enforced learning of subjects and memorization of theorems, chemical formulae etc. We were not encouraged to think outside the box as the recommended textbooks were our cardinal compass and absolute truth. The passage of time brought the realization that memorizing chemical substances and history dates did not provide life skills. It was evident that experiential learning and the process of personal growth and development came from transforming, adapting, and embracing change. Jalaledin Rumi's poems aptly articulate lessons learnt from experience.

"We can't help being thirsty, moving toward the voice of water. Milk drinkers draw close to the mother. Muslims, Christians, Jews, Buddhists, Hindus, shamans, everyone hears the intelligent sound and moves with thirst to meet it."
Jalaledin Rumi

Rumi's poems help one understand the inner depths of our consciousness, the nature of being human while yearning for the Divine, and to prioritize what is important in our lives. His significance in history is not just in Sufi Islam, as he has touched millions of others, and is one of the most-read poets in the West...perhaps more so there than in Muslim societies. Rumi's thoughts align with both the private spiritual search that many seek, as well as with the speeches and Farmans to the Ismaili community made by His Highness The Aga Khan. The Imam has stressed the use of the intellect, to accompany this search, both to live our lives fully and ethically, and for faith to be understood rationally.

Older now, we realize that the deeper spiritual dimension of life and its importance were not ones we paid attention to, beyond the obligatory daily prayers. That was perfectly normal at that age. But as we reflect on our lives, and our parents and their devotion to faith, much more is understandable about their actions, decisions and worldviews...and how they have shaped us and our personalities. We may not have succeeded as well in influencing our children as their environment is not a small city, but the world, and the communication revolution allows them to listen to multiple voices on any subject, often opposed to our own views. Indeed, life was much simpler in Nairobi of the '60s.

Poem on Remember
by
Joy Harjo

Remember the sky you were born under, know each of the star's
stories
Remember the moon, know who she is
Remember the sun's birth at dawn, that is the strongest point of
time
Remember sundown and the giving away to night
Remember your birth, how your mother struggled to give you
form and breath.
You are evidence of her life, and her mothers and hers.
Remember your father. He is your life also.
Remember the earth whose skin you are: red earth, black earth,
yellow earth, white earth, brown earth, we are earth.
Remember the plants, trees, animal life who all have their tribes,
their families, their histories too.
Talk to them, listen to them, they are alive poems.
Remember the wind. Remember her voice. She knows the origin
of his universe.
Remember you are all people and all people are you.
Remember you are this universe and this universe is you.
Remember all is in motion, is growing, is you
Remember language comes from this.
Remember the dance language is, that life Remember all is in
motion, is growing, is you.
Remember language comes from this.
Remember the dance language is, that life is.
Remember.

Kenya~ Contextualized

Vasco de Gama recorded seeing Indian merchants along the coast of East Africa in the late 15th century. Kenya's dominant tribe are nomadic pastoralists, the Masai warriors having a reputation for conducting fierce raids, which gave them power beyond their numbers. The largest tribe is the Kikuyu who live primarily through subsistence farming. The early 19th century met with an influx of Arab traders in search of ivory and their settlement in Zanzibar, spreading Omani Arab culture to the coastal towns and the city of Mombasa. The British Government established its protectorate in 1920, encouraging European settlements to the prosperous fertile temperate highlands, later known as the White Highlands. Most of the settlers came from South Africa and introduced forced African labour on their farms. A railway was needed from Mombasa to Kisumu, for which 30,000 Indian workers and traders came from British India.

Kenyan Politics

The establishment of the colony of Kenya introduced new legislation on land tenure favouring the settlers. The Kikuyu tribe was the main loser to be dispossessed of the best farming lands to white settlers. Indians and Africans demanded representation as white settlers were allowed to elect 11 seats to the legislative council in 1920. Indian strength in economic and negotiating power won the right to 5 seats, with one seat for an African member.

The number of token African politicians, appointed by the colonial governor, reached eight in 1951. The lack of representation, dispossession, marginalisation, and discrimination led to the Mau Mau rebellion (1952-1960), with acts of terror perpetrated against the settlers, and with even more violent responses by the British.

The colonial government declared a state of emergency and arrested Jomo Kenyatta in 1953, leader of the Mau Mau movement, with seven years of imprisonment. During this period, 916 Asians, 200 British soldiers, and 32 European settlers were killed, whilst 20,000 Kikuyus were killed as collaborators or in prison camps. British domination was not to last as independence movements were spreading across Africa. A conference in London in 1960 gave Africans the majority of seats in the Legislative Council, leading to the formation of Kenya's first African party. Jomo Kenyatta was elected President of the KANU (Kenya African National Union) party, whilst still in detention. In December 1963 Kenyan Independence was achieved with Kenyatta as Prime Minister and he was elected President in 1964.

Independence brought a period of volatility in African and Asian relations as in 1967 Immigration Act requiring Asians to acquire work permits, whilst a Trade Licensing Act limited trading areas. Faced with a dim future, many Asians who had opted for British passports at independence, chose to move to the United Kingdom.

Kenya demographic & Socio-culture

Kenyans have 13 ethnic groups with minorities comprising Asians, Arabs and European accounting for less than 1% of the population. Significant Indian migration began following the creation of the British East African Protectorate in 1895, which had strong infrastructure links with Bombay in British-ruled India. The majority of Asians trace their ancestry to Gujarat and Punjab. Languages spoken by Asians include Gujarati, Hindustani, Konkani, Kutchi, Marathi, Punjabi and Sindhi.

After the Second World War, Asians were found in all occupations in Nairobi with their commercial skills contributing to the economic development and prosperity of Kenya. Despite accounting for less than 1% of the population, their businesses dominated Main Street. Prior to independence Asians owned three quarters of the private non-agricultural assets in the country.

The Indo-Trinidadian writer, V.S. Naipaul, commented that the East African Indian brought India with him and was inviolate, cautiously inward and self-reliant. The Asian population was estimated to be 44,000 in 1931; 179,000 in 1962; 139,000 in 1969; 78,000 in 1979; 47,000 in 2009 and 46,791 (Asian, Arab, European) in 2018. In 2017, Uhuru Kenyatta's government announced recognition of Asians as the 44th tribe in Kenya.

Religious practice is important and more than half the population constitutes of Christians. The Asian community is mainly Hindu, which includes Lohanas, Lohars, Rajput, Patels and Mehtas, among others. The next largest community are Muslims, the majority being Sunni Muslims; however, there is a significant Shia minority, including Ismailis, Bohras and Ithnā'ashariyyah. Islam is the main religion for communities living along the coast. Smaller numbers of Sikhs and Jains are also present.
A handshake is the most common greeting and a sign of respect. "Jambo" or "Habari" (How are you?). "Kwaheri" (Bye). Kenyans have a casual approach "Hakuna Matata" (No problem) to getting any work done.

School Life
by
Cheryl Theseira

School is a daily routine for us
In the morning we're sure to make a fuss.
Even when the sun is still not up,
Here we are awake at 6 am sharp.

Late a minute and we have to run
Eyes half open, shoe laces undone
We see our friends and the torture ends.
We may at times find school stressful,
But go with the flow.
To have some fun we have to bend the rules
Even knowing we are fools.
So much learning from experiments and activities,
And knowledge based creativity.

Some may find school a torture chamber
Some cannot wait for the holidays in December,
But it depends on how we look at school,
Honestly, positively, school was cool.

School Life

My education during the colonial days was based on the British model. The pressure to make career choices was inflicted at completion of Standard 7 when we were graded in our KPE (Kenya Preliminary Exams) at age 12-13. A poor performance or failure meant compromising a decent education, whilst students with the best grades were admitted to four years of high school, commencing with Form 1. The top 33 were in the "A" tier, whilst others were admitted to "B", "C" and "D". Being an "A" student alleged you to be bright and given the opportunity to study Latin, French, Physics, Chemistry and Biology, in addition to English and Maths being subjects available to all.

At the end of four years, based on results, 16 students were admitted into Arts or Science each, for two years of "A" levels. In 1967, when we wrote our "O" level exams, our career choices were made at ages 16-17. Many of us enjoyed good grades in maths, chemistry and biology but performed poorly in physics, which barred us from the top 16 into science for "A" levels. The flexibility for career choices accorded students in current times is a better system.

I am a Muslim woman and have been a product of a co-educational system from nursery to high school. During our school years there was no discrimination in gender, as females were treated no differently in the quality of education provided. I strongly support this system as it worked towards mending the gap between genders, building a bridge of friendship and enabling confidence through life in dealing with male cohorts at university or work. My comfort level in studying with boys was never an issue; in fact, it instilled a sense of healthy competition. Furthermore, upon entering colleges and universities I felt no anxiety at having to study with male colleagues. Later in this book, I identify a teacher whose instruction favored boys, but this was a particular teacher and not the system. Unfortunately, this teacher's prejudice impacted our career choices unfairly.

Our school motto was in Latin 'Ad Augusta per Angusta' meaning to rise to a high position overcoming hardships. We proudly wore our green school blazers with an embroidered crest using gold wire sewn on red wool to reflect a top quality crest. In addition to the blazer crest we could wear green cardigans, green ties with red stripes symbolizing Ismaili colours, green for joy, gaiety, prosperity and peace, with red connoting sacrifice.

Prior to independence, fear and awareness of the Mau Mau movement was pervasive. My recollections of this time of terror are vivid as our house was in a valley and a possible target. Those curfew years met a revised schedule at home, a quick change in clothes to prepare for dad's arrival to push heavy furniture against the doors. My father's sudden possession of a gun, with no skill to use it, was scary, and I fervently prayed every night that we would never need it! No play time, no mosque, no friends - just fear of the unknown!

Despite this fear, we were assured that we lived in safe colonial times with the Queen in power and a tough police force. We had seen pictures of the Queen as reigning monarch reflecting her beauty, elegance, expensive attires and obvious ruler of many colonies. Being brought up in this era, we celebrated colonial events like visiting the Royal Show, on Ngong Road which after independence, became known as the Royal Agricultural show, showcasing Kenya's industries and businesses.

The Royal show allowed a day off from school to appreciate well-bred cows, goats, sheep\sheep shearing, chickens, pigs, coffee beans, tea, flowers, with the top three farmers being recognized for having the best in each of the categories. Many businesses offered free samples allowing us to take home bags of goodies. Bands marching in procession and rides made for a day of fun. After independence, we were not allowed a day off school or free entrance to this event, and our attendance met with its predictable demise.

To celebrate the Queen's birthday, we were given an official holiday from school and went to the same grounds on Ngong Road. As we eagerly approached the grounds we watched Her Majesty's Parade of military guards in immaculate uniforms, mounted police on horseback with a regalia of colours, a gun salute marking her age, Union Jack flags for every attendee and a day of festivities and fun. Throughout Nairobi, buildings were decorated to honor the Queen, including the Ismaili Jamatkhana.

As children, the Queen, general politics, policies, and recognitions did not feature in our lives and had little meaning except for the anthem recited during morning assembly and later having to learn the new Kenyan anthem following independence. After Kenya's independence we mounted Kenyan flags, and hung portraits of President Jomo Kenyatta in our school, homes, and mosques, alleging our loyalty to the President and country. Our new currency contained images of President Jomo Kenyatta, which replaced those of the Queen. Our adoption of the Kenyan anthem was seamless and we adapted quickly.

"O God of all creation
Bless this our land and nation
Justice be our shield and defender
May we dwell in unity, peace and liberty
Plenty be found within our borders.
Let one and all arise
With hearts both strong and true

Service be our earnest endeavour
And our homeland of Kenya
Heritage of splendour
Firm may we stand to defend."

Nairobi was a beautiful safe city with excellent weather. Every day offered spring conditions with sunrise at 6.30 a.m. and sunset at 6.30 p.m. Luxurious school buses promptly transported us from the areas we lived in to school, for assembly with teachers, students and prayers at 8 a.m. The Principal and teachers took their places on stage whilst students were part of the general assembly, required to stand in line with their classes.

Some of the female teachers attending our assembly mornings were single, good looking, wore mini-skirts (attire of the times) and high heeled platform shoes, a treat for the boys. Good looking female teachers were thin, porcelain complexioned, walked with elegance and enjoyed good composure. Boys would salivate as Ms. Lal, gorgeous, beautiful and well-poised, entered the assembly hall, attired in designer clothes. Arguably, she did not realise the havoc she caused but must have broken many a heart when she married. School ended at 4 p.m. with return bus transportation to our respective areas of residence.

School bred disciplines like, efficiency, competitiveness, meritocracy, determination, and success. As teenage girls, influenced by Mills and Boons and Enid Blyton books, we dreamt of a knight in shining armour sweeping us of our feet, two children, a nice home and a decent social life. A dual-income family unit was part of our thinking as we wished for a life with social and material plenty, fun, conversations with friends, and a happy ever after.

The final outcomes defied imagination and were not remotely close to our dreams. In our class of '67 and '69, emotional bonding and friendships at school were rare but present, and three couples dating at school forged matrimonial ties. Despite our fun and games it was generally easier to excel at academics and suppress attractions for later in life. This did not dismiss multiple and varied feelings and emotions that were felt by many students.

Our personal lives and emotions typify stories of young people proud, happy and hopeful. Being attracted to the opposite gender was natural but we dismissed feelings we could not understand. In the '60s, only boys could declare their attraction for girls, thus relegating girls' emotions to secrecy. Chances of mutual attraction were remote as girls generally became attracted to boys smitten by others. As we had never experienced romantic feelings, our first love made us believe we really cared as we transposed perfectionism onto the images of our crush. Secret crushes, were one-sided upheavals tantamount to nothing! Fast forwarding to our current age and time we wonder if we should locate our high school crushes, we would probably laugh at our immature choices.

Aga Khan High School, Nairobi, in the '60s had physics and chemistry labs, a large multi-purpose hall, swimming pool, two sports fields and basketball court. School facilities were considered the finest, providing a great learning environment. Benjamin Franklin stated that the only thing more expensive than education is ignorance. As a woman, I think of the huge number of women who are deprived of an education because of their religious persuasion, personal or financial circumstances. At Aga Khan High School, we were privileged to enjoy the best of education without realizing our good fortune. His Highness Prince Karim Aga Khan's luminous vision at this one school enabled education for an estimated 500 students a year. Over a period of six decades it changed 30,000 lives and impacted as many families!

Currently, the Aga Khan's pragmatic provision of education and compassion for all, irrespective of caste, colour or creed, has more than 240 schools under Aga Khan Education Services providing pre-primary, primary, secondary and higher secondary education to over one million students between 5-18 years of age in Africa, Asia and the Middle East. The Aga Khan Education Services is one of the largest private, not-for-profit, non-denominational educational networks in the developing world. The Aga Khan Foundation, with UNICEF, is developing digitalised stories and curating interactive platforms to enable literacy skills for children.

Despite attending an Aga Khan school our medium of instruction and language spoken with friends had to be English, failure to observe this requirement resulted in a medal at the end of the day. Adopting English-only rules at school was onerous as we were so accustomed to a mix of Kutchi/Gujarati with English, and receiving a medal suggested violation of the English-only rule and a fine of 25cents, which we could ill afford. Our effective Machiavellian machinations had to be unleashed on unsuspecting classmates. This was a short-term band-aid solution as classmates smartened to the devious games and we were compelled to speak English without the use of our vernacular, conceding to the administration's wish.

The medal system was an example of the impact of colonial rule and its governance, instilling a belief that everything English was superior and we emulated a western concept of speaking, dressing and listening to music. At home I spoke in Kutchi or English, whilst communications with my grandmother were in Kutchi, as she spoke no English. Food and religious practices were unaffected and continued as normal. Religious instruction was provided but due to the non-denominational status of our school, this subject did not impact our grade.

Communication with my grandmother poignantly reminds me of a majestic matriarch to be obeyed. She lived in a large landscaped home, entertained heavily and was regularly adorned in expensive jewellery and quality clothes with the luxury of a driver, cook and housekeeper, living the life of a wealthy bourgeoisie. Despite not having had an education, she was a strong-willed intelligent woman influencing decisions in her extended families and households. Once she was widowed and embezzled financially, her life changed significantly.

From her shouting quality-control instructions in Swahili to her staff of four:
'Hapana! Sitaki' No, not acceptable or 'Nenda zako' or begone, she struggled to cook and clean her small apartment. As a widow with constrained finances, her attire and lifestyle was simple as she spent her day gazing out of a window with tasbih (rosary) in hand as widows generally accepted lives of solitude and surrendered to remembrance of God upon the loss of their husbands. Although not destitute, as upon her demise her Canadian property was bequeathed to her grandchildren.

by
Elizabeth Cady Stanton (1)

If the sexes were educated together, we should have the healthy, moral and intellectual stimulus of sex ever quickening and refining all the faculties, without the undue excitement of senses that results from novelty in compartmentalized isolation.

Journey through Co-education

Chinese philosophy for at least 3,500 years states our universe and nature have been governed by a cosmic duality of energies, and the two opposing complementing energies of yin and yang. Yin is an inward female and male is the masculine outward energy. If nature is shaped by the duality of energies it is regrettable that we have built obstacles in allowing women fair access to education.

My thinking concurs with Elizabeth Cady Stanton, who was disappointed by the education provided at the female secondary schools in 1865 around the time of the American Civil War. Early feminists feared that separate education for women was inferior to that of men and the only way of ensuring equality, they argued, was to insist that women and men be educated together.

Sultan Mahomed Shah, Aga Khan 111 (1945) is quoted saying "If I had two children and one was a boy and one was a girl, and if I could afford to educate only one, I would have no hesitation in giving the highest education to the girl." This vision statement provided girls' high school education in the '50's at the Aga Khan Girls High School in Nairobi. This foresight not only provided an operational model to deliver a good standard of education for girls but impacted their professional aspirations with a quest for seeking employment opportunities and changed their approach to nurturing children. Primary education in the '50's adopted the correct direction in encompassing dual energy into our academic system. I am a product of a co-ed system of education at the Aga Khan schools in Nairobi. We were an anomaly, frowned upon and, arguably, watched as test projects to allay fears for this type of education ushering an onslaught of negative consequences. Being a Muslim and attending a co-ed system was not a favorable trend in the

60's, as single-sex education was prevalent in many Muslim schools and countries. The Aga Khan promoted co-education through all levels of learning from nursery to high school and most Ismailis supported this system with highly successful outcomes.

Co-education appealed to the leaders of the early women's movement, not simply on academic grounds but on sexual grounds as well. In their view, the segregation of young men and women led to an undue preoccupation with sex; whereas the joint education of the sexes created a more natural and therefore healthier sexual atmosphere.

The trend toward co-education is gaining popularity amongst many countries including Pakistan and India, and is now being adopted by almost all countries globally. This system has many pros and cons based on the way it is adopted, implemented and utilized in the educational institutions. However, critics of the co-education system still argue that students get distracted and diverted from studies to indulging in undesirable activities. Their beliefs are based on fear of risk of teenage pregnancy weakening the academic foundations of the school and a student's future. They allege that the co-ed system of education promotes distractions and they strongly support an all-boys or girls school to erase activities damaging student lives.

My journey through co-education never presented the fears expressed. In fact, I looked forward to going to school and enjoyed the academic learning, which allowed my development and growth to thoughts of equality, irrespective of gender. The negatives expressed were not present and not an issue as my co-ed system of education was natural and I am a product of an integrated education system from nursery school to University. Having to recount my journey through co-education, I was surprised at the natural speed in summarizing the advantages bulleted:

- Formulating healthy and confident relations with the other gender.
- Providing for a fun social environment.
- Respect and equality for every individual, irrespective of gender as learning needs are the same.
- Excelling in class as I learnt the views and opinions of the opposite gender.
- Being an adolescent in High School, it was only natural to be attracted to the opposite gender in class or school. If in the same class, I was more driven to impress them through academic performance and this did instil competitive spirit amongst genders.
- No feeling of awkwardness towards opposite gender especially when communicating, presenting thoughts and debating in front of class.
- Claims of distractions for the other sex may be true but equally strong was the need to concentrate and focus on the subject. Ultimately, transparency of my grades to the class made it even more important for me to excel academically.

I attribute my social and emotional success to understanding relationships of my co-ed experience. From a very young age I played and have studied with the opposite gender, and strongly attest to an education system where academic co-ed environments encourage students to think and embrace learning, guided by excellent teachers. At Aga Khan Schools, we were privileged to have an academic strategy which vouched for excellent teachers preparing us for life in an interconnected world. Our teaching faculty had been carefully selected and many times expatriate teachers were hired at high salaries and benefits, if local recruits were not found.

Research conducted by the Strategic Counsel, a Toronto-based market research firm that interviewed 17,798 high school students in 2006, published its findings in a report, *The Benefits of the Co-educational Environment*. Students reported greater confidence expressing their views in the presence of opposite-sex peers than those from single-sex environments. They stated they were more likely to make friends with members of the opposite sex, and they reported lower levels of harassment and bullying than their single-sex peers. After all, real life is about accepting plurality, diversity, and encouraging students to appreciate mixed energies, as opposed to silos and compartmentalized thinking.

Hope
Vaclav Havel

Hope is not the conviction that something will turn out well but the certainty that something makes sense, regardless of how it turns out.

Walt Disney

We keep moving forward, opening new doors, and doing new things, because we're curious and curiosity keeps leading us down new paths.

Age of lingering Innocence

"I don't want to repeat my innocence. I want the pleasure of losing it again." — F. Scott Fitzgerald

Pretentions of confidence, upon arriving at Aga Khan High School, Nairobi, at age 13 were masked by fear, trepidation and hopelessness. All other students were older, the school was new as were rules and some classmates. Unlike in primary school, we now gravitated to hang around classmates similar in age and in the same classroom. Although High School suggested a need to act grown-up and establish our identities, at heart we were deeply overwhelmed, frightened and confused. The challenges of a new school were daunting and at the end of day we gratefully raced to the comfort and security of our homes and parents, away from our tumultuous days at school.

What happened five decades ago in Kenya seems surreal and unimaginable. Albeit, social patterns change depending on what's current but we too were influenced by class and schoolmates in our fashion trends and behavioural patterns. An age of limited resources restricted our ability to readily be influenced by trends but as young people we had the energy, mindset, and social need to project change.

Our parents chose and planned our daily lives but we had the verve and ability to squeeze fun outside of everyday school, homework, and Jamatkhana. The key factor was our attitude; we were content and happy with our lives (we knew no better and were oblivious to adult lives and responsibilities). Our teenage years allowed us to look forward to times of freedom of choice, not realizing that time, youth and vitality, once spent, were never to be retrieved. For us teenage innocence was taken for granted. In a blink, our lives changed and it was hard to explain, understand or know, what forces brought this sudden upheaval as we scattered to institutions of higher learning amidst different social and cultural norms. Growing freedom and social life experiences brought the realization of having lived our teenage years in lingering innocence and ignorance.

It is difficult to imagine Aga Khan High School, Nairobi, to have been devoid of wild parties, teenage pregnancies, drugs or negative social issues. In fact, these were abhorrent and stigmatized. Teenage innocence was natural as the city and our community was small, trusting, respectful and protective of the young. We were sheltered and unaware of what teenagers know today. Despite being in a co-education school, we were ill-informed and lacked understanding the facts of life, as we avoided exchanging information on what we considered a taboo subject. It was a perfect time for parents, as they took pride in their children being educated whilst facing few to no challenges in their upbringing and social norms.

Our teenage years were synonymous with an ardent desire for school romances, expected teenage crushes and infatuations. Social events added greater sparkle to dormant feelings at becoming love-struck. This passion had to be dismissed as a fleeting emotion, infatuation to fade with growing years and the realization to being more in life than physical attraction. Sexual repression seemed to be the norm whilst the freedoms of the Baby Boom Generation were unknown to us.

When in Form V, we felt licensed to a new-found freedom and our supposed maturity. Most poignant was early morning entertainment by a cast of two: Yasmin Gulamani (Jivy) and Nazmudin Jiwa (Flat Bottomed Flask. FBF). Jivy was a beauty, akin to a Greek Goddess - thin, tall, green eyes, brown hair, Aryan complexion, high cheekbones and

46

elegance to match her looks. Nazmudin was tall, boisterous, and confident with an exaggerated sense of arrogance.

FBF loved Jivy with profound intensity and every morning pledged his undying love threat of first killing himself and then her! His dramatic threats vouched to take his life first and after his death still have the ability to take hers! Every morning he would not only publicly declare his love but would have some endearing or threatening remark. Jivy, not to be overpowered, had smart rebuttals that left him trodden. We, the audience, were amused, entertained, and wagered bets on FBF ultimately winning Jivy's emotion. Jivy was not to succumb to this public display and despised him for his behaviour.

Form V1 brought added responsibility of being prefects to watch over and discipline juniors. Prefects were appointed to enforce rules according to the British school system. It was incumbent for prefects to be exemplary and we attempted to be strict and intimidate juniors. For a period of a month, I was overseeing a class one year younger to me and Late Zahir Madhani (Kalulu) sang the song Delilah, changing the words to my name: "Why why why dear Naila?" I suppressed my laughter, admiring his guts, courage and originality and spared him punishment for his behaviour.

Despite having created playfulness, this was not universal as the demand for excellence was pervasive and integral. In our life journeys, the healthy blend of work and play prompted a similar ethos in the organizations we created, communities we lived in, and the children we raised. Excellence and discipline were well-ingrained and provided a fascinating mix of self-confidence, decisiveness, intelligence, articulation, being well-informed, critical, and analytical in our problem-solving, all with a sense of humour and jest. Our enigmatic teenage years, though baffling and spent in lingering innocence, suddenly became lucid during our reunions, with widespread success stories of hard work and discipline.

Our adjustment to the High School environment was innocent but boisterous, well-behaved but mischievous, respectful of elders but politely wanting time with friends listening to the radio, records, going on picnics, travelling, enjoying study soirees, getting ready for parties at one house or another, hitch-hiking but ultimately remaining focused on academic success. Forging bonds with friends at school and university assumed importance but with a difference. School friendships continue to this day, assisted largely by attending religious observances at Jamatkhanas, and the need to have helped each other in our settlement processes in the countries of adoption.

My recent diagnosis with cancer and toxic chemotherapy treatments reconnected me with an ex-class mate, Nilofar Karim (Rayani) from High School, living in Orange County, California, who travelled twice to Calgary and patiently looked after me during treatments, providing care for two weeks after 50 years of disconnect! It was normal for me to stubbornly reject any visitors or phone calls but surprisingly an exception was made for Nilofar.

Hilarious ~ punishment for an errand

We shared literature books with Form IB for a specific reading and Mrs. Hetherington sent three boys (Firoz Jiwani, Sadaat Kheshavjee and Firoz Gulamhussein) from our class to carry books from a class next door. Form IB was close to finishing their reading and the boys were requested to wait outside the class. In the interim, we were engrossed reciting Mrs. Hetherington's favourite poem, Nkosikasi's Keys - certainly not politically correct today:

"Wherever have they got to?" she says with a wrinkled brow.
"I left them on the table and they've simply vanished now."
So cook must leave his baking and the houseboy on his knees,
A-searching under things to find Nkosikasi's Keys.

Mr. Buckley, our assistant Headmaster, was on his rounds and ardently played his role in inviting the boys to his office and caning them with no opportunity for explanation. Upon remembering the three missing boys sent on an errand, Mrs. Hetherington went to their rescue but a little too late, as the punishment had been delivered. The class and Mrs. Hetherington experienced waves of laughter, with no sympathy for the victims' pain, humiliation, and sullen looks. The following morning, in our general assembly, Mr. Burke apologized to the boys, but the class laughter and teasing lasted many years. Corporal punishment was administered to maintain discipline, and the false assumption of boys standing outside due to misbehaviour met with immediate action. It was not permissible to cane girls, although we could be slapped with an open hand. How times have changed! But I cannot say this form of punishment had any lasting effect, other than a grudging and reluctant respect for authority.

Bet

The Quadrangle (quad) was a rectangular open air space surrounded by classrooms, labs and stairs leading to classrooms on the upper and ground level or to the assembly hall at the lower level. This quad was the center of activity and held a special significance for annual school photos to be taken in this courtyard. It was intended as an area for contemplation, study, or relaxation but we preferred to meet and chat with our friends. At the time we did not realize that universities provided quads, and we were fortunate to have been blessed with a quad in our school.

Boys had a tendency to congregate and sit under the stairs at the quad. We soon observed the reflecting objects in their hands to be mirrors, as they glimpsed exciting views of girls' underwear as they climbed the stairs. Upon realization of this travesty, we sneered at their short khaki pants and disgusting hairy legs and challenged them to introduce respectable long trousers worn by "A" level boys. Upon admitting failure in their request for change they challenged the girls to bring change in our uniforms.

We eagerly accepted the challenge. Fortunately, the Administrator's daughter, Nasim Teja (Rashid), was not only in our circle of friends but a classmate, and we approached Mr. Crockery, our Principal, for a change in uniforms. He was hard at work to ensure that Nasim had no cause for complaint and was quick to comply with our wishes, with a caveat that Mrs. Lopez, responsible for the girls, approved our request. Our new design had a couple of pleats in the back and front, was easy to wash and iron, and presented a look of consistency, irrespective of how the skirt was maintained. The cost of purchasing new skirts was a hurdle she could not overcome, but became accommodating upon suggestions of a phased approach. Our success was a big win for the girls, proving that boys could be outsmarted.

The continued fetish for trousers led us to unforgiveable misdemeanours. Not to miss school buses soon after PE (physical education), boys would carry trousers in their hands wearing their PE shorts. Long bus rides would have them napping and give us the opportunity to throw their khaki trousers from the bus to poor and more deserving people. Our naivety did not consider the costs involved and inability of these boys to afford a replacement. We never got into trouble as the boys were too embarrassed to report their loss.

A poignant reminder was Alnoor Vellani (Bushbaby), a sinfully good-looking but shy senior from Mombasa who failed to acknowledge our smiles which we mistook for snobbery. His sullen looks and ignoring us was not only impolite but discourteous and to be reproached. His PE group called Chui (Leopard) delayed him one afternoon and he fell victim to our long awaited action. He had his trousers on a seat next to him and fell asleep allowing us to toss his trousers outside to a waiting youth. The certainty of performing good deeds for the poor and needy allowed us to be free of remorse.

Free Lunch

One of our classmates, Azim Popat, painfully shy and quiet, was the son of a wealthy owner of Simba Motors. He was nicknamed Gopi and harassed every birthday for a free lunch in the school canteen. Unfortunately, his birthday would not fall on Fridays when our favourite fish and chips would be on the menu. Hence, Mrs. Akbarali, our canteen manager was familiar with our annual request for fish & chips on Azim's birthday. She was a wonderful lady and agreed to serve the dish on a day other than Friday as it made business sense.

Coco-nut candies for free

Sadaat Khesavjee was known to bring a bag of coconut candies to sell, but our pocket money did not extend to the luxury of purchasing some. His first desk on the right side, was one desk away from the aisle to the wall. Thus, whilst he attentively listened and took notes we availed of his candies by passing his bag through the aisle to the last two desks at the back of the classroom. We were only allowed two candies per person and by the end of class his bag would be next to his desk. His mother kept adding to the supply source until she wanted revenue for the sales. Depleting candy supplies with no revenues was a surprise to Sadaat, and caused him to tie his bag handle to the leg of his chair. His action brought our short lived candy supply to an end and put us in pursuit of our next adventure.

Hitching

By the time we were in Form 111, we had the smarts, intelligence and panache to pull off greater adventures. Our inner circle of friends totalling, six or more, would hitch rides to the Westlands shopping centre bakery shop for delicious strawberry tarts, at a cost of one shilling to be shared amongst us for a small bite of the tart. Three rules for this adventurous activity entailed staying together (imagine 7 girls hurled into the back seat), hitching for luxury cars (preferably Mercedes) and confidentiality of our nefarious activity.

Were the tarts just an excuse for the excitement of hitching? A Judge in his Rolls Royce gave us a return ride, as we excitedly got into his Rolls Royce, I was seated on someone's lap and decided to check the curls in his ceremonial-wig, unaware that he could see my action through the mirror in his car. He humorously enquired if his wig was of an acceptable quality? One time, Mumtaz Ebrahim's (Karmali) uncle stopped in his Mercedes to give us a ride and Mumtaz implored him to not tell her mother. He bought us each a tart and took us back to school. I suspect Mr. Hossein, our Principal, had been tipped of our perilous activity and once he stopped in his lemon-coloured Mercedes and took us to the centre for a tart each and brought us back to school. He informed us that our brilliant grades, teachers praise and success in extra-curricular activities did not merit punitive action but we had to help set up his daughter's birthday party the following day. Everything, including silence, has a price.

Walks to meet friends

Our school holiday walks from old Highridge to Parklands became more frequent and predictable. The late Farida loved to wear tight leggings with short tops and walk on the outside of our group on the tarmac road. This was likely to attract attention - and it did. One of our walks met with boys in a red car smacking her rear with force as we heard the loud smack, her scream, and watched her fall to the tarmac with a frightened face, tears, pain and anguish. Totally confused, we did not know whether to laugh or empathize….. uncontrolled laughter ensued! But she was unhurt…...just a bruised ego…..

by tree.cards

School is something,
we must all embrace.
Knowledge we need,
to seek out and chase.

Subjects and teaching styles,
are plentiful and vary.
Just like the bags,
we all need to carry.

Sports, clubs, and activities,
at every single turn.
So much to do,
study and learn.

To get the most from school,
we should consistently attend.
Around each corner,
there's always a friend.

Our favourite teachers,
are friendly and kind.
Their passion and job,
to expand every mind.

School is something,
we must all embrace.
Just remember to learn,
at your own pace.

School Classes & Activities
Musical Productions

Amy Patel was talented and had the ability to turn a plain shy girl, into a shining star on stage. She was the rock of our High School drama club and excelled in her reputation for musical productions to packed audiences. She played the piano remarkably well and brought the audience to life with plays such as Fiesta and Carnival in Cacao.

Despite being new entrants to High School, her selection of Form 1 students to star in Fiesta with seniors, was not only a source of great pride but caused us to praise this production as being the best this world has witnessed. Fiesta was an indelible hit with the students and audiences begging for more. We were certain that Amy Patel was more talented than Richard Attenborough. The play converted our Assembly Hall into the setting of Mexico with colourful costumes, dances, senior boys in charro suits and senior girls in poblana dresses, whilst junior boys in indigenous skirts and junior girls in poblana dresses made from layered black netting with bright red piping. All costumes and stage sets were stitched and designed by Amy.

Amy's next production was Carnival in Cacao, where I was her heroine, dressed in the lovely long dress worn by beautiful Leila Esmail, in Fiesta. This dress had been stitched to accommodate Leila, but at that time, it was the best dress I had ever worn! Once again the Assembly Hall was transformed with lighting, sound effects, piano music and bongos, which enhanced the production.

Carnival in Cacao was capturing Carnival time in an island in Brazil with blue skies, sandy beaches, palm trees and where love and laughter dwelled all day. Tourists from Hong Kong, France and Japan were featured. Most costumes from Fiesta had been recycled adding kimono styles, sophisticated French attires and tropical dresses appropriate for the visitors. In this production, the novelty of an airport arrival lounge on a raised dais, to the left of the assembly hall where girls with binoculars excitedly waited for the arrival of their loved ones with a welcoming song set to Brazilian drum beats and Calypso music welcoming all to the land of blue skies, laugher and swaying palm trees. This musical production had at least eight great songs but to infuse nostalgia for the glorious past two poignant songs may revive fond memories:

Men Smart, Women Smarter

Chorus line:
Ah Not me! But the people they say
That the men are leading women astray
But I say (I say) that the women of today
Smarter than the men in every way
That's right the woman is uh smatah (4)

Coconut Woman

Coconut woman is calling out
And every day you can hear her shout
Get your coconut water...Coconut
Man its good for your daughter....Coconut
Coco gotta lotta iron....Coconut
Make you strong like a lion....Coconut

Amy Patel's popularity placed added pressure on her to introduce better productions outdoing the previous ones, and her creativity rose to the challenge. Despite the overwhelming pleasure of a great applauding audience and Amy Patel's tepid encouragement for professional acting, creating a passion for drama would never have met with parental approval and had to be suppressed. In the 60's it may have been glamorous for those who found success but was generally considered an unstable career choice incapable of steady income. Ironically, she had taught our class a song that lingers to this day as we live and work in urban cities.

Bingo, Bingo, Bongo I don't want to leave the Congo,
oh no (4) Chorus sung twice.
Bingle, Bingle, Bungle I don't want to leave the jungle
I refuse to go.
Don't want no bright lights, late nights, hot spots, tough Scots don't want them all, for the jungle is the place for me it keeps me busy as a bee and free.

Physical Education

By the time we were in Form 111, we had synthesized knowledge and insights into a lot of school activities, including PE, which was physically demanding. We found solutions to not running our cross country in its entirety as we took a shortcut to a small hill, where we sat and chatted. Our chatter was generally shallow, fake rumours and any matters of interest. Upon sighting the slowest male runner, Shiraz Dossa, we commenced our run. Not getting caught was of importance and we were smart to evade any trouble, but seemingly small actions such as this have never enticed me to exercise or jog for health or vanity to this day!

Other girl sports entailed swimming, 100 & 440 yard sprints, hockey, netball and rounders (baseball). I was a swift sprinter and excelled at long distances but lost the agility soon after school. Girl sports were not competitive nor taken seriously, but allowed us to appear sporty for a while.

Religion

To this day we regret not having taken our religious studies seriously due to our non-denominational school and its exclusion from our overall grades. Our teacher, the late Mr. Hassan Nazarali, tried his best to impart religious knowledge and we tested his patience. He was a tolerant, kind, even-tempered, composed and stoical individual. Religious exams were always the last and we never studied for it as our celebratory moods were set on having completed other exams.

Once again, our machinations for writing religious exams demanded creativity, as we wrote intriguing snippets from his teaching and a lot of Shakespeare from Julius Caesar, Othello, Romeo and Juliet and The Merchant of Venice as example of afflictions of general human qualities e.g. "If you prick us, do we not bleed? If you tickle us, do we not laugh? If you poison us, do we not die? And if you wrong us, shall we not revenge?" (The Merchant of Venice Act III, scene I). From Othello, our use of themes of betrayal, jealousy, general love, racism, and revenge provided adequate and varied grounds to respond to questions.

Our school participated in the annual waez (sermon on religious topic) and ginan (devotional hymn recitation) competitions. Waez competitions consisted of the late Farida, Mumtaz, and myself to win trophies, three years running. The Ginan competitions had Nasim Teja (Rashid) participating. It was an honour to win these competitions as they were provincial and a source of great pride for us, the school and our parents.

In addition, our religious education instructor controlled the appointments for students Majalis Mukhi/Kamadia Sahebs and Mukhiani/Kamadiani Sahebas for a period of one year. These appointments supposedly trained youth on the performances of our Jamat khana rituals. Students attended these prayer sessions once a month on a Saturday evening in a central location at the Town Jamatkhana. The place was packed to seating capacity as it accorded students an opportunity to meet and socialize. The girls' hostel students were transported to these majlises which provided an added incentive for guys to attend. This also allowed the girls to plan their wardrobe choices to look their best. With great pride, the late Azim Mawani/ Mehdi Janmohamed and Naila Abdulla/Nasim Karmali (Kassam) as appointees assumed positions of responsibility.

Physics

Our Physics teacher, to be nicknamed Mr. Physics did not disguise his disdain for girls studying the subject, and in his heavy Indian accent, belittled us with offensive comments as we were "phit" for domestic science. His dislike was transparent, as he strictly taught boys, with total disregard for the girls. He knew the boys by their names and refused to acknowledge girls' existence even when we attempted to answer his questions. His huge bulging belly was exposed through ill-fitting shirts with popped buttons, and his shirt failed to remain tucked in his loose fitting pants. Even if he knew physics, his mannerisms were disgusting as he used a dirty handkerchief to aid him draw a perfect circle on the board, he wiped his nose on his shirt sleeve and his huge under arm perspiration mark was visible. It is hardly surprising that girls decided to boycott his test in Form 1V, hoping to gain empathy from our principal. Unfortunately, our brave action met with a reprimand for our belligerence and we bid farewell to any chance of pursuing a career in science.

Final "O" Level physics grades for most of the girls were poor and disappointing and compelled us to pursue arts for 'A' levels. All was not lost as we sought revenge whilst in Form V. Our Economics teacher to be nicknamed Mrs. Economics wore a *chandlo* (red dot on the forehead) and saris. We learnt she had no children and was desperately seeking to have one. On Valentine's Day, Mrs. Economics received a card from Mr. Physics expressing his hidden adoration for her and fervently wanting to give her a baby. Our class room was next to the staff-room and we heard her quick steps storming to the Physics Lab to smack Mr. Physics on his face (we learnt of this from students in the lab). He was shocked as was his class at Mrs. Economics rash outrage. We had paid a big price for his discriminatory behaviour but by sending the card we sought to be avenged!

Literature

The study of literature was separate from that of English and the stories provided utilitarian real-world skills. Whilst English class coped with grammar, essays and vocabulary drills, our Literature class enjoyed a special allure because of our teacher. Mr. Elias, was from Southern India, had an abnormal gait, and his heavy black shiny shoes warned us of his arrival long before he arrived but his love for literature was contagious. He always stood at the first desk next to the teachers table and never ventured into the class.

Nasim Karmali (Kassam) occupied the first center desk and laid her pen, pencil and ruler on her desk, ready to take notes if needed. Mr. Elias had become accustomed to fidgeting with these aids whilst exuding his love for English Literature with passion and losing himself in the process. Sharing his love for literature was marked with a raptured class intently listening and enjoying the passage of time. His frequent one minute smile, exposing white teeth against a dark complexion, had us wondering if his thoughts were subject or personal-related.

His fidgeting had Nasim distracted and at a loss for patience, putting away her pen, pencil and ruler, hoping he would find another desk. Mr. Elias, was not to be swayed from this front desk and continued to stand at the desk he was accustomed to. At the end of one class, his shoelaces had been tied between the two shoes, confirming a fall from any movement. He managed to remove his shoes using the teachers table for support, undoing the shoes once seated on his chair. The class was amused, but he responded kindly, with dignity and a smile, thereby winning greater affection for him and Literature.

The Third Planet
© Naqiya H. Shehabi

When you see the green mountains,
And feel the lush valleys,
Know that they're all yours.
Cherish them; the more you will,
The more you'll be thankful,
For the time you spent between them.

As you look over the blue waters of the ocean,
Remember to smile.
Look out for the fish swimming.
Embrace this beauty,
For all it is ours and ours only.

When you look upon the shining stars,
Be eager to know how they were made.
Learn about space and time.
Treasure the grace of the burning orbs,
And then create a connection,
For they resemble your love.

As you peer into the grassy plains,
Look out for the mighty lion.
It has a better eye than you do
And a roar mightier than you've ever heard.
If your eyes ever get a chance,
Glance toward the sky,
For it shows what we've got.

This is not all;
The beauty on Earth is widespread. Learn to respect it,
And it'll embrace you instead.

Trips & Travelling
Serengeti, Ngorongoro & Manyara

School trips were organized for graduating classes of "O" and "A" levels in celebration of completing benchmark studies. Two buses to transport 30 students in each bus were rented. "A" level and "O" level buses were separate and each bus was assigned 4 adult chaperones. Rules for the chaperones were simple as student monitoring against alcohol, and illicit drugs was not an issue, and neither were considerations of safe water, food intolerances, health precautions, visas etc. The cost was nominal and itineraries were pre-set for "A" level to Manyara, Ngorongoro, and Serengeti game parks and "O" level to visit Sereneti, Manyara and Ngorongoro.

Although we lived in Nairobi, for many of us this was the first time to experience the savannahs of the Serengeti, views of Mount Kilimanjaro, the famous Ngorongoro crater, Lake Manyara with its tree-climbing lions - the excitement and overall feeling was overwhelming. Letting our imaginations run to experience the wild and untouched beauty of seeing the Masai in their habitat or the full range of African wildlife, including lion, cheetah, elephant, giraffe, rhino, wildebeest, zebra, gazelle, possessed our thoughts, dreams and talks.

Before getting to Serengeti, our first stop was Arusha, a small town in proximity to Mount Kilimanjaro. Cousins and friends residing in this town extended a warm invitation to an afternoon party, which we graciously accepted. Parents in Arusha heard of this plan and forbade their children to entertain the big city of Nairobi kids. Unaware of Arusha parental displeasure, we excitedly descended upon Arusha for our afternoon party. Upon arrival, it became evident that arrangements were poor as a small VW was to transport 30 students to a party 10kms away. Multiple trips got us to a dilapidated location with a record player, records, soft drinks and crisps. We spent more time on the crammed round-trip

VW transportation than the party with adverse consequences to our return time.

Our driver indulged in drinking local brew for his afternoon and was stopped by the police for his hazardous driving before we left Arusha. We were detained under curfew until early morning when the driver would be sober to operate the bus. Our curfew location was a snow-cream parlour, belonging to an Ismaili who kindly allowed us the use of his premises for the night. The police stressed we were permitted to be on the bus, in the snow cream parlour parking lot or the parlour, and no further. Detaining a bunch of 16 year olds to a restricted area is untenable. We tried to follow instructions but at 10 pm, became restless and we descended to cross the street to the Hassan Auto store driveway where we danced to guitar music supplied by a couple of classmates. Residents above the store launched a complaint and the police walked us back to our curfew location with a warning and reprimand.

We had not planned for this discomfort and were unable to sleep. Arusha Jamatkhana was within short walking distance and we craved a hot cup of tea with cookies, served to the early morning meditation attendees. At 3.00 a.m. we ventured out and saw volunteers preparing tea and were informed to return in an hour directing us to wait in the adjacent hall where social events and final rites for funerals were performed during the day. A coffin was placed on the stage, visible to us patiently sitting across in a state of tiredness. Firoz Jiwani decided to experience lying in a coffin whilst alive. Watching him stand resulted in loud shrieks, piercing fearful cries and a race out of the social hall. Angry adults at the Jamatkhana refused to serve us tea, compelling our despondent return walk to the bus, regretful - of our stop in Arusha which had deprived us of our chance to visit Serengeti.

Disappointed, downcast, sad, and tired we walked across the large parking lot when one of the girls saw a flock of white-winged terns, and this renewed hysterical screams. It only took one person screaming to illicit contagious screams from the rest. Unfortunately, residential flats surrounding the Jamatkhana complained of disturbance and the police walked us to our bus. I do not believe the Arusha Police had ever had a busier night than keeping an eye on us. Our behaviour deeply distressed the chaperones, who repeatedly fell asleep every time we had stepped away from our curfew area. In fact, one of the chaperones tried to distribute his Marlboro cigarettes to placate the police and managers at the lodges, which prompted the composition of our kutchi lyric promising bribes of Marlboro cigarettes to all when troubles erupt:

"Hi kuro, ho kuro, panke kuro". What is this, what is that, it's of no concern to us.

Our departure from Arusha met with a sigh of relief and sleep at the news of being fortunate to resume our tour of Serengeti National Park. To annoy our chaperones, we resumed singing a popular song by Manfred Mann transformed into our lyrics, Do-Wah-Diddy met with: "Do what daddy did to mummy to get me"

Basic dorm accommodations with outdoor latrine facilities at Ngorongoro was a welcome change, after our dashed Arusha trip. Conventional behaviour amongst a gang of 10 girls or more escorting one person needing to visit the washroom prevailed. In this instance, Nasim Teja (Rashid) was being escorted with the torch being placed in her hands. She opened the broken door to the already occupied latrine by Mamdif Jiwa, and kept flashing the torch aimlessly in the pitch dark to his nervous voice alerting us of his presence. We saw nothing but claimed to have seen it all, much to his embarrassment through the trip!

70

After our failed mission to use the washroom we decided to inspect the dorm and use the latrine on our return to the dining-room at the lodge. Our dorm visit surprised two of our chaperones intimately engaged, and we opted to blackmail the female who worked at our school. Our blackmail allowed us access to the staff-room standalone mailbox. Additional surprises were almost impossible on this short trip, so we happily resorted to singing, snacking and enjoying our time when the wheels of our bus went round and round onto a muddy dirt road near Lake Manyara. No amount of Marlboro cigarettes were to let us out of this ditch! Soaking wet and fearful of wildlife attack, we pushed with all our might using muscle power but to no avail. We were lucky to have had another coach push us out of the ditch to drier ground.

Late arrival at the Aga Khan primary school, drop-off and pick-up point, was met with worried and concerned parents at the stories "A" level students had spread venomously about our Arusha arrest. Our parents were gratified to see us and placated as we assured them of the hugely magnified exaggerations the "A" level had spread. It was not in the interest of our chaperones to complain as they were in charge. It was almost impossible to describe our incredible, once-in-a-lifetime travel experience as we tearfully bid farewell to some who were not to return to school for "A" levels due to restricted admission compelling them to pursue careers not requiring "A" levels.

Trip to Mombasa and Malindi

Allaudin Bhanji visited his mother in Mombasa every holiday, so I procured essential details from him on travel requirements and imparted these details to my friends for the possibility of a roundtrip to Mombasa at shs.10 - about three dollars. The cost of travel appeared cheap and had to be verified with a classmate from Mombasa, Faiza Kanji, who wore a huge wrist watch (symbol of affluence) and she willingly imparted detailed costs of her train travel which matched those of Allaudin. They traveled first class, whilst we were willing to rough it sharing a second class compartment.

For eligibility we needed a parent in Mombasa, the school Principal's approval, and had to complete forms attesting our parents lived in Mombasa. Our late friend Farida Hasham's father was a bursar and upon his lunch break we pretentiously entered his office looking for him. Whilst Farida kept his assistant, Johnab, busy we stole 6 blank forms and stamped them with the high school stamp. Mumtaz forged our Principal's signature, as her dexterous handwriting skills could create identical signatures. Each of us completed the forms with correct parent names and Mombasa as the city of our parents domicile. Parents were oblivious to our treachery but generally consulted other parents in granting permission for any social events. If Yasmin's parents consented then mine would and so would Farida's and so on.

Having hitched a ride to the railway station to buy our tickets we faced a long line, in which a couple of teachers and the Principal stood. We dared not show our forms and insisted we were there for information. In the line was the late Ali Sinuff, who invited us to a cottage he had rented in Malindi. After our teachers departed we purchased our travel tickets and excitedly prepared for our inexpensive trip to Mombasa as we had to reside with our respective Mombasa relatives.

Waving our parents "au revoir" from the train station platform, we embarked on a 15 hour steam train journey on the "Lunatic Line" to Mombasa. The train departed at 6 pm with a whistle and a thud as its engines cleared for overnight travel to arrive at Mombasa by 9 AM or later. Our cabin attendant was contacted for a bed berth in exchange for the enormous amount of food our parents had packed. We were aware of the railroad having been built by Indian labourers at the turn of the century, and the terror of 100 of them being killed by lions. The engineer, Colonel James Patterson, in his book "The Man-eaters of Tsavo," relates this narrative while the movie "Out of Africa," in its opening scene provides images of a steam train travelling across the Tsavo plains.

As the train whistled through Nairobi suburbs, we finally relaxed to the realization of being on the way to our Mombasa adventure. Pre-dusk suggested we had limited time to enjoy the view as darkness set us for a night journey of songs with an imaginary guitar accompanying Petula Clark, Dionne Warwick, Aretha Franklin, the Beatles, Cliff Richard, Elvis Presley songs and discussing plans for our Mombasa trip.

Mombasa is situated on Kizingo Island on the east coast of Kenya along the Indian Ocean. The city is known as white and blue, I surmised because most buildings are painted white against the blue ocean backdrop. It is the country's oldest city with a mix of Portuguese, Omani Arabs, Swahili and Colonial cultural influences making this city alluring and incredibly enigmatic. A visit to Kibokoni and Kuze allowed immersion in Swahili, Omani and Baluchi cultures, transporting us to the land of Sultans, Emirs and burqas. Imagination runs wild as you wonder how thrilling it might be to see everyone and not be seen by them, enjoying the total anonymity of a burqa. Thoughts of the heat, and the garment being suffocating or stifling were absent as bemused notions predominated of tricking people in Nairobi by wearing a burqa.

Taking the Likoni ferry was a must as it validated our trip to Mombasa whilst swimming in Bamburi beach, feeding oneself coconut, cassava and mangoes made the trip complete. Our tastes were simply founded in enjoying the cultural influences, without understanding the historical impact of what we enjoyed. Despite the kindness and hospitality of our relatives, we missed our friends. Meeting friends became an arduous and challenging task due to distances and respecting the wishes of our relatives' plans for local sightseeing.

We decided to go to Malindi and stay with Ali Sinuff at his rented cottage. Spending money was short, we barely had shs. 30 each and decided to take a local bus to Malindi. As we boarded a packed bus never used by Asians, some Giriama women occupying the side bench seats gave us their seats. We sat in shock staring at the topless Giriama women who returned our stares, and laughter between us ensued. We discussed their shapes and sizes and they must have found us strange in skin colour and alien attire, never having experienced our type on their bus. Our travel took us on a ferry crossing with an on time arrival into Malindi. Fortunately, we found the cottage before Ali, a teacher Mr. Hasham (Dhingli), his wife, and Mark headed for dinner to the Eden Rock Hotel, a five star resort on the beach. On our budget we had pledged to a cardinal rule of never talking about food or hunger. We changed in a minute, ready for our evening escapade to the plush Eden Rock Resort.

Our arrival at the resort at dinner time meant ordering dinner, we unanimously stated we had eaten and ordered Coke, attacking bread baskets to empty no sooner they were put on the table. We danced the night with Ali, Dhingli and Mark, had a fabulous evening and returned to a one bed-room cottage with its washroom being separated by the bedroom occupied by Dhingli and his wife and a veranda occupied by Ali and Mark. We now occupied the veranda, having to go to the washroom through the bedroom which was unacceptable to Dhingli's wife. Sharing her husband's dances with us had been painful and now the loss of privacy was the final straw. We needed to use the washroom and tried to whisper so as not to disturb them but she was angered and adamantly insisted on our eviction the next morning.

Feelings of hopelessness descended as we had nowhere to go and limited funds. Encouraging each other to be calm under stress was our first line of action as we sat on the sandy beach with our luggage, listening to the waves and enjoying the heat of the sun. We consoled ourselves at having a full day ahead for an alternate search and found a rest house using bunk beds that was not only affordable but could accommodate six at shs.18 per room, including breakfast. We opted to stay three nights to enjoy and swim in pristine clear beaches in Malindi. After all, our main reason for being in Malindi was to connect with nature, laugh and chill with friends, feel the sun, sand and sea. We respected our rule to dismiss thoughts of food except when a street vendor would sell us cheap coconuts.

Despite our practice of emptying bread baskets from all tables as a norm to feed us through the day, Yasmin Dossa (Mohammed) and I could not resist the supper menu offering chicken curry, rice and chapatis. We confidently walked to the owner and asked her the price of the full menu which was shs. 3.00. We enquired the cost of curry and rice; curry and chapati; chapati only. The lady invited us to sit at the table and served us a full meal in a large bowl of curry, lots of rice and chapatis.

Our friends, with curlers in their hair came looking for us due to our prolonged absence, finished the remaining food and left just before the owner re-entered the dining room. Both Yasmin and I were tiny fragile beings and the owner's shocked expression spoke volumes as she pityingly commented on our extreme hunger and did not charge us for the meal.

Our nightlife (clubs & discothèques) was possible contingent on ordering a glass of Coca Cola each for the entire evening. Fortunately, there were no cover charges and we danced till our feet hurt. Many attractions located in Malindi's proximity had to be ignored due to our budget restrictions. Not being able to see the Gedi ruins offering Swahili and Arab cultures or visit the Arabuko-Sokoke Forest Reserve harboring elephants was a travesty not to be forgotten.

Our wonderful days through Mombasa and Malindi were too short and as our travels ended, we thanked God for having blessed us with an authentic, incredible fun opportunity abounding in fond memories to last a lifetime. Upon our return, we felt guilt and remorse at our treachery and worried about public humiliation in case of Police arrest. We held our truce to never reveal the truth to other friends or parents of forging forms for low cost train travel. Life has enabled many travel trips to several exotic countries to best resorts and travel comforts but the simple fun enjoyed at low cost travel as teenagers tops the list.

Mount Kilimanjaro Expedition

By Firoz Rhemtulla

At the Aga High School Nairobi, there was an annual tradition. Every year the new class of Form Fives would attempt to climb Mount Kilimanjaro, a dormant volcano in Tanzania. It has three volcanic cones, Kibo, Mawenzi, and Shira. It is the highest mountain in Africa and highest single free-standing mountain in the world at 19,340 feet.

The Science and the Arts classes of Form Five were grouped together to form the expedition. This group was divided into Troops of eight or ten students and each troop had a leader. Mr. Tamana, our strict teacher, was the esteemed leader of the expedition. Much to Mr. Tamana's dismay I was selected as one of the troop leaders. I remember a few of the students that were in my troop; Mumtaz Karmali, Hasan Shapi, Mohamed Noah (Shifta) and Nazmu Jiwa.

Climbing Mount Kilimanjaro is a strenuous undertaking that requires stamina and endurance, plus you have to be in good physical shape. The air at the summit is very thin and it's a grueling effort to make the last dash. It is a four or a five-day adventure to ascend and descend the mountain.

Mr. Tamana had put together a strict training schedule to prepare us for this physically demanding adventure. We used to do cross- country runs behind our school on a regular basis. If I remember correctly, it was a three-mile loop and quite hilly. We also did overnight trips to Mount Longonot and Ngong Hills. Mt. Longonot is in the Great Rift Valley and stands at 9,100 feet. Besides climbing the mountain, we also hiked around the rim which is a four-and-a-half-mile loop. We also hiked the Ngong Hills, peaks in a ridge along the Great Rift Valley.

Unfortunately, my troop got into a lot of mischief - except for Mumtaz Karmali. We were not very good at following rules or obeying instructions from Mr. Tamana. I believe I was the instigator; we made our own rules. We were up late at night when we were camping. We used to sit around the campfire and smoke cigarettes - except for Hasan Shapi. We were late getting up in the morning and I was not the best leader to get my troop organized for the day's outing.

Mr. Tamana was livid and I am sure he was ready to throttle me. He would have hit me if it were not for Mohamed and Nazmu, who were big boys. I would like to think that they would have stood up for me.

Heading home after one such trip, Mr. Tamana had the bus driver pull into the Ngong Police Station. He asked Hasan, Shifta, Nazmu, and I to follow him into the station. We were stunned and had no idea what was going on or what he was trying to accomplish. Perhaps he was trying to scare us into behaving ourselves. We walked up to the counter and he told the Police something that none of us heard. The officer pulled out his large ledger and proceeded to take down statements from each of us. He started out with our names, ages and what we had to say for ourselves. When he came to Hasan Shapi, he asked if he was related to Gulu Shapi. Hasan replied that Gulu was his father, who happened to be the Chief Police Inspector for the Ngong Region. The officer decided to call Gulu Shapi. All we could hear at our end was "Yes Sir, No Sir, unha.":

When he hung up, Mr. Tamana asked him what that was all about. The officer said Gulu Shapi wanted to know if his son had committed a crime. When the officer said "no" Mr. Shapi told him to let the boys go and not to bother him with trivial matters.

Needless to say, Mr. Tamana was furious as we strode back to the bus, proud as punch. Unfortunately, that was our last involvement with the Kilimanjaro Expedition; we were expelled from the expedition.

I want to shout out to our teachers. We are where we are today because of their passion for teaching and their dedication to mold and groom young minds. I owe an apology to Mr. Tamana for making his life difficult; I was young and cocky and I thought I was invincible.

Just Dance!
Tree.card

It doesn't take much,
to simply begin.
And let all of it go,
that's building within.
It's just like a switch,
that sweet sounding tune.
Never too late,
and never too soon.
Shoulders and hips,
instantly sway.
Bringing forth,
a beautiful day.
With the right partner,
or mutually alone.
Moves arrive randomly,
the next is unknown.
To enjoy fully,
don't seek a reason.
As long as there's music,
there's always a season.
Don't look around,
or shyly glance?
Whenever you feel it,
remember - Just Dance!

Parties & Celebrations
Parties

End-of-term exams and the pressure of studies, met with a celebration dance at the Aga Khan Primary School hall, organized by Firoz Kassam (Hitler). Firoz was known for organizing term-end parties, was a year senior to us, and organized these social events despotically, as he assumed responsibility and accountability. He was nick-named Hitler as he exercised total authority on the students invited, songs to be danced to, hours of operation etc.

Parties, prom, celebrations, and school had a common thread weaving through the events – our friendships kept us energized and connected. In preparation for the party, our circle of friends gathered at a friend's home to attire in our doll dresses. It was essential for our entry and exit from the dance hall to have strength and solidarity so we arrived and left together. Fear of being a wallflower was remote, as convention did not encourage more than two dances with the same partner (even if you liked the guy) for fear of sending a wrong message. If the couple was dating, the rules did not apply.

Competition between Cliff Richard and Elvis Presley clubs was common, but in addition, we enjoyed the Beatles, Rolling Stones, Aretha Franklin, Roy Orbison, Supremes, Neil Diamond, Engelbert Humperdinck, The Shadows, Monkees, Bee Gees, Santana, Animals, Stevie Wonder, Chuck Berry, Herman Hermits, Neil Seidaka, Everly Brothers, The Hollies, Peter, Paul & Mary, The Drifters, The Ventures, The Mamas & Papas, Bobby Darin, Four Tops, Crosby Stills and Nash.

We danced the jive, twist, cha-cha, disco dancing and two step slow dances. Sometimes, visiting cousins from England performed the latest dances in England by demonstrating their moves on stage to a host of young eager imitators ready to mirror every grimace, nuance and body move. In addition, we frequently displayed our knowledge of proficiency at dance through a series of small gestural actions in a steady rhythm previously practiced. We enjoyed Latin and African-American influences known for being fast and fun.

Celebrating our Imam's Wedding

The fall of 1969 was a precursor to our final "A" level exams and was met with study schedules and strategies to ace exams. A surprise announcement of Imam's wedding to Begum Salima was released, and with it our resolve to respect study strategies assumed secondary importance. The excitement and fervour was magical as our mothers bought expensive materials to stitch clothes for this special occasion.

Special celebrations are marked by pleasing all the senses. Instead of using air fresheners, my mother would pluck fresh jasmine flowers and place them on our centre table in the living room for a gorgeous sweet fragrance. In addition, oudh wood chips were burnt providing a sweet deep fragrance of patchouli and jasmine to the entire house and our clothes. Having prepared myself with new scented clothes, I was ready to celebrate! I love the lingering scent of oudh in my clothes and house and have become attached to the practice of burning oudh on a regular basis and indulge myself to the use of oudh in my home, bed linen and towels to this day.

Preceding the wedding we participated in ten days of nightly celebrations at each of our Jamatkhanas with music, food and dances after prayers. Frantic attempts for best decorations at each of the Jamatkhanas were assumed whilst teams of cooks assembled to prepare exotic menus for each evening. Volunteers worked 24/7 to ensure clean premises, organized serving of food and beverage, adequate dandias (sticks for dances) and myriad of responsibilities to ensure a great celebration.

For Ismailis, any celebration is community-centered; hence, Ismailis globally celebrate special occasions according to varied traditions, communal preferences, and culturally appropriate menus. Nairobi, in 1969, was predominantly composed of Khoja Ismailis with a mix of Sindhi, Kutchi and Gujarati cultures. As teenagers we were ready to party from dusk-to-dawn playing dandia/raas demonstrating our grace, agility and energy as we revolved almost into a trance like dervishes to the amazing music.

Our celebrations and dances were open to all ages and dance abilities but friends found a spot where we could dance freely with style, coordination and free of speed restrictions. Novices or individuals who could not keep up to the required speed were avoided and labelled as disruptive. It was crucial that everyone maintained the same step and beat, as failure to observe the rhythmic flow would adversely impact the dance bringing it to a stop.

We generally danced dandia/raas in concentric circles with repetitive movements increasing speed as the dance progressed. Raas was performed by clapping twice or three times, with the third time clap involving a twirl. Dandia is a stick dance and we waved colourful sticks with special style and swirls in graceful and rhythmic movement to hit sticks of our rotating partners. For added style, we would hold both sticks in one hand using the free hand for expressions whilst we happily danced to the music of our favourite band, the Flames, who in our opinion were unmatched in the catchy music they played. Our favourite was a Hasidic song, Hava Nagila, which solicited screams of approval loud singing and dancing with fervour.

Any interruption, even to partake in dinner, was an intrusion and infringement on our dance-time. Despite our initial objection to any interruption, once we were at the food tables we ate whole-heartedly and did justice to the not-to-be-repeated menus of appetizers, dinner buffets and desserts served nightly! The food was delicious and every evening we guessed at the possible menu for the next day. The day of the wedding served samosas, sev, biryani and ice cream faluda. Sev and faluda were rich with nuts as we were not aware of nut or lactose allergies at the time. Every night we were served sherbet, cake and cookies.

To ensure variety and amusement for the seniors there were skits and performances of singing and dancing. Closer to the wedding day, a mehndi event was held for women to adorn their hands with intricate henna designs. These designs were considered cosmetic, and our school did not permit student beautification. The rules were strict and we were expected to wear our hair short or tightly tied in a pony- tail, short nails free of varnish, no rings or earrings, as Mrs. Lopez stood at the Assembly Hall doors to conduct random checks on our hands and hair to ensure no violations were attempted. Surprisingly we were not affronted by this extremism on an occasion very special to us as it allowed more dandia time. Henna decorations take time to design and dry. The celebration was magical, dreamy, amazing and extraordinary.

Prom Night

Prom night celebration was a privilege reserved for Form V1 to mark the end of High School Journey marking an end to our youth becoming adults. Glamorous Prom Night was in December, after our "A" level exams and before we entered colleges and universities in September of the following year. The Designated committee responsible planned for an exceptional Prom at the High School Assembly Hall. The mood was set as the space had been transformed with prism lighting hanging from the high ceiling, round tables in a semi-circle around the dance floor, fresh flowers, cloth tablecloths, napkins and chairs draped with gold-coloured cloth. A live band was on stage, whilst our then Administrator, the late Dr. Gulam, the Principal, and class teachers were interspersed at our tables. It was a night to be remembered and brought the realization of a benchmark chapter of our lives meeting closure. Promptly after mid-night, our school buses drove us to our respective residential areas for the final time.

Rumi

One form of intelligence takes shape in acquiring knowledge, while the other comes from within. You can be sure you'll forget most of the contents in your high school textbooks but that doesn't make you any less intelligent. Because there's an existing library within you, filled with intuition, experiences, and most importantly, is one that is mouldable to change. Share your life Share your life lessons with the world. It's the one kind of intelligence that truly matters.

Two kinds of intelligence
There are two kinds of intelligence: one acquired,
As a child in school memorizes facts and concepts
With such intelligence you rise in the world.
There is another kind of tablet, one
Already completed and preserved inside you.
This other intelligence does not turn yellow or stagnate.
It's fluid, and it doesn't move from outside to inside
Through the conduits of plumbing-learning.
This second knowing is a fountainhead
From within you, moving out.

Plagued by Questions & Life decisions

As young adults we did not realize that life would have many crossroads and transitions. Going abroad in quest of higher education was one and it exposed us to a multitude of cultures, traditions, religious beliefs, social behaviour and cultural shocks. We had arrived at a critical juncture where new knowledge brought tough questions on how one might maintain stability in making choices. The comfort of our home, mosque and conformist life-styles had led to a world of pluralistic values and a frightening chasm between the present and past. At school we took most of our learning and what we were taught for granted, without asking questions. Away from our cocoons we asked questions, not knowing if they were the right questions to ask.

Rationalizing the importance of our character and personality, our questions were logical in wanting to know: what is my character? What is my personality? What actions can I permit so as not to dislodge my personality, character, traditions and faith? How do I relate my new social activities to new classmates, friends and society? What is moral? What is ethical? What are values? My past is of no consequence to the culture I am in, and I am too inexperienced to determine the right mix of integration. Personal independence was great but immaturity made us ill-equipped to answer daunting questions on coping and managing our freedom.

At age 18, questions were simple, thinking was naïve with unanswered questions leading to more questions. Since childhood, almost every question was met with an answer related to God. In a vacuum, questions abound: who is God? Where is He? What is my relationship with Him? Who knows Him? What is the purpose of my life? What am I to do? How we wished we had taken our Religion classes more seriously. To add to my confusion, I had not read the Quran but understood it to provide 'clarification of everything' (16:89) and a set of guiding principles to be applied appropriately through comprehension and contemplation ~ a skill I lacked.

Adding to confused religious understanding, there were more personal questions relating to: Why is my skin olive-coloured? Why do I eat and enjoy different foods which I can no longer get? Why is my mother tongue not spoken here? What am I doing in England and why me? How different am I really from the rest? In a world of confused responses we succumbed to living life as best as we knew how, getting focused on academia and accreditations, for that was our purpose for being abroad. Passage of time brought social mobility and adjustment was no longer defined by culture but by countries we lived in.

I questioned having postponed my dating for later years, as it bypassed my teenage experiences. Since childhood, my life was shaped by cultural expectations of the Kenyan Ismaili community; hence, our string of accomplishments in academics, and later in financial security, were important. Maturity brought a different world view and I questioned the values on which I was raised. I surmised on the shallowness of our customs, thinking, gender inequality, judgemental thinking and sought answers where none were to be had. I thanked God for our playfulness at school and a life free from monotony as I concluded there was nothing wrong with harmless and innocent fun and laughter.

The freedom and lifestyle of my new circle of friends was definitely not acceptable by our cultural standards, but acceptable by the standards in England. This experience made me question our sexual repression, relationships we had failed to develop in our teenage years due to the moral standards of our society. Amidst a plethora of questions, I found myself anchoring importance to being just, honest, showing respect and responsibility. Any momentary remorse I felt evaporated to the reality of financial pressures due to currency restrictions imposed by Kenya, forcing me to budget carefully and look for jobs during holidays.

Upon reflection, academic pressure and teenage years run parallel and tough choices have to be made. Why is our academic system taking so long and costing so much to prepare a student for a jobless market? University education prepares us for entry level jobs with the employer having to train and prepare hires for the job. Is our system of education flawed? Is our system of education dated? If early childhood education is important in a child's development, then why should an individual spend 25 years of their prime life acquiring an education? Are the number of years spent in acquiring theoretical knowledge acceptable? Could this process be reduced in the time spent? Is the education system's attempt to conform to student lives causing more harm than good? My experience taught me greater life skills than the classroom.

What is globalization? Is the concept well understood by all? Maturity brings wisdom, realities and experiences to better understand that globalization upsets known cultural, religious, philosophical and judicial traditions that even modernity issued from the reason of the Enlightenment does not escape (Mohammed Arkoun, What is Globalization?). In fact, Europeans speak of the limits and perverse effects of globalization and mounting tensions. As an immature student, I was oblivious to notions of pluralism, globalization and diversity, as I sought answers and struggled with a different culture and geographic region. With the passage of time I recognized my confusion to be part of continued learning. I consoled myself that life was to change as soon as I graduated and returned to a land of familiarity. My graduation meant a return to Nairobi to a life of my dreams and my childhood.

Front Door
by Imtiaz Dharker

Wherever I have lived,
walking out the front door
every morning
means crossing over to a foreign country.

One language inside the house,
another out.
The food and clothes
and customs change
The fingers on my hand turn
into forks.

I call it adaptation
when my tongue switches
from one grammar to another,
but the truth is I am addicted now,
high on the rush
of daily displacement,
speeding to a different time zone.
Heading into altered weather,
landing as another person.

Don't think I haven't noticed
you're on the same trip too.

Kenya loses Sparkle

Independence brought a period of volatility in African and Asian relations as in the 1967 Immigration Act, which required Asians to acquire work permits, whilst a Trade Licensing Act made operating businesses difficult. Faced with a dim future, many Asians with British passports chose to live in the United Kingdom. During my student years in England, in 1972 I was shocked at the news of Idi Amin, President of Uganda, having expelled all Asians. Idi Amin cited the Uganda Indians to have exploited the local economy and failed to integrate with black Africans after a century in the country. In his "Asian farewell speech" in August 1972, he accused Asians of "economic sabotage." I had friends who were traumatized and gave up their studies due to inability to pay fees and having to financially support their parents and siblings.

Upon completion of my studies, as a proud and excited graduate I returned to Kenya, overjoyed to be reunited with my family, relatives and friends. My excitement crushed to an unexpected disappointment that was hard to accept. Although I had a job with a British tour operator in a scarce job market, advancement opportunities were poor. The country was unsafe with looting and attacks, as Kenya's political context had domestic tensions, abuse of power, and high levels of corruption. Its key development challenge included poverty, inequality, a weak private sector, and a vulnerable economy dependent on tourism and agriculture.

The Uganda crisis had seeped into Kenya and Tanzania as fearful Indians fled, even though there was no imminent political threat from local regimes. Most of the Ismailis were Kenyan citizens and did not have the option of leaving Kenya for England like other Asians holding British passports. In my early 20's I lacked business savvy for development opportunities, which at the time provided limited opportunities for Asians. Childhood dreams had been ripped in a blink of the eye, as the chasm of incompatibility between country and citizen grew wider and changed forever. Feeling betrayed by my motherland, my life was in chaos as I felt lost, alone, abandoned and forlorn.

Having often heard that change provides an opportunity for personal growth and development, I still brooded privately trying to think of solutions that would marginally introduce change, and allow me to stay in Kenya. Tourists continued to visit Kenya for it's game parks in Masai Mara and pristine beaches in Mombasa oblivious of the hardships brewing for its diverse population. Kenyan Indians no longer felt welcome in the country of their birth and were treated derogatively with the expression, Wahindis, which defined Asians as mean and exploitative business people. Most Asians fearful for personal security installed burglar alarms whilst news of Indians being robbed, killed or homes being burglarized were common.

My asset was an English education with limited work experience, proving to be worthless in Kenya, compelling a broader search for opportunities abroad. Fortunately, employment applications for start-up jobs in England and Canada met with positive results accompanied by settlement prospects. As a young person with no hope in Kenya due to anti-Asian sentiment, unemployment crisis, oil-shocks, graft, and tribalism at a fever pitch, it was time to leave. What hurt the most was a life-long dream had been shattered and I was in crisis mode.

Who likes to leave their home land? Leaving Kenya was not an action to be taken lightly as I was aware of the difficulties abroad from my years in England, but critical thinking coupled with advice from elders suggested emigration. Our forefathers had crossed an ocean in unsafe vessels and invested their life blood in enriching Kenya. I was expected to give up what they had worked for and the hardships experienced, but with a difference. Our modes of transportation were safer, I had an education, had found a job and was headed for Canada, an industrialized country, with better standards of living. A decision to leave Kenya, my family, relatives and a life-time dream was highly stressful. Indecisiveness prevailed as persistent concerns for my future life prevailed. A decision to leave was forced by circumstances that I took unwillingly. In addition, currency restrictions allowed meagre funds to begin life afresh, not enough for the purchase of winter clothing necessary. Thoughts reverted to Ugandan refugees whose homes and properties had been forsaken with generations of work in a suitcase and no choice over their future country, gave me strength to move forward.

Migrating from country of birth to becoming a citizen of Canada brought many challenges of diverse cultures and social norms. I learnt to share a sense of 'otherness' with those in similar circumstances. Experience suggested that whatever the differences, being different was difficult but it opened a wonderful possibility of being rich in a complex heritage of cultures and a willingness to adapt. I had become adept at embracing change, coping with being different and establishing strong foundations.

Thanks to Canada's humanitarian and compassionate family considerations, I sponsored my father, grandmother and younger brother, settling for a life of responsibility unthinkingly, giving my best to the future of family, country and community. As a responsible adult, I embraced a life of hard work, honesty, compassion, frugality, helping others in need of help, assisting families settle in their new homes and continued education to advance in my workplace.

As a newcomer with humble roots, I proudly embraced Canada as my home and became an integral part of the fabric of Canadian society. In a relatively short time, my hard work met its reward as I assumed a leading role as an executive in a charter airline, being the first minority female. As an executive for leading tour operators, charter airlines, car-rentals, retail agency, and hotel organizations, I pioneered initiatives that introduced Nordair to Florida, Canadian tourism to China, Cuba, Cancun, Ixtapa and the Dominican Republic. I was instrumental in developing contractual agreements with resorts in the United States, Canada, Mexico and Caribbean, always mindful of sustainable development in the tourism sector. I was appointed as a member for The Ontario Travel Industry Compensation Board and represented Canadian Charter Airlines for the North American Free Trade Agreement.

Work advancement met with honorary nomination in the community and the privilege of being a member of the Ismaili National Council for Canada. I was privy in the late '70s to be one of the pioneering members of FOCUS, an NGO that provided food, shelter and education for 1,200 hundred orphans and marginalized children in India. FOCUS's initial mandate met with a change in the '90s to emergency relief. I was a fundraiser in 1985 for the opening of the Ismaili Centre, Burnaby, (a powerful symbol of Ismaili permanence in Canada) and subsequently the Aga Khan University Hospital, in Karachi, the Aga Khan Rural Support Program in Gujarat, Hunza, Gilgit and Chitral. As Chairperson for the Economic Planning Board of the Ismaili Council, an assistance program was established for empowering immigrant women from Afghanistan. My aspirations and thoughts to positively impact humanity globally for a peaceful and equitable world continue.

Rumi

Unfold your own myth
*Instead of living vicariously, how can you live a life that is truly
yours? Because there is no day in a calendar that is not there for
the taking — for you to proclaim carpe diem. You can live your
dreams instead of dreaming to live. You need only to align your
purpose with yourself.*
Not a day on any calendar
My Life Is Not Mine—
Give up wanting what other people have.
That way you're safe.
"Where, where can I be safe?" you ask.
This is not a day for asking questions,
Not a day on any calendar.
This day is conscious of itself.
This day is a lover, bread, and gentleness,
More manifest than saying can say.
Thoughts take form with words,
But this daylight is beyond and before
Thinking and imagining.
*Now it's easier to follow a common path that has a track record for
"success". Unfortunately, there are more lost souls coming and
going from this path because it was actually never meant for them.
Everyone has a unique voice, but not everyone can sing. Forget the
success stories you've read before you. It's time you
unapologetically unfold your own myth.*

But don't be satisfied with stories,
How things have gone with others.
Unfold your own myth,
Without complicated explanation,
So everyone will understand the passage,
We have opened you.
With such intelligence you rise in the world

Achievements

Esmail Merani

In an attempt to capture past achievements of my years at high school I recall numerous classmates, friends and senior students achieving sporting or academic success. In the '60s, meritocratic success took effort, courage, skill, academic brilliance and hard work to attain achievements. Two of my classmates, Mehboob Karmali and Allaudin Bhanji, set records of excellence for 'O' and 'A' level exams. For 'O' levels, despite a vast range of subjects in conventional academic subjects, they attained the highest grade in each subject and later, for 'A' levels, achieved A in each of the science subjects. Arguably, it was not only the best our school had ever recorded but the best by any Kenyan standard. Bright students normally are a small minority, but a majority of 'A' level students gained acceptance at universities due to good grades, ability and motivation. This further validated and distinguished the school's standard of education and quality of its teaching faculty as remarkable.

My life journey was influenced by the Aga Khan High School (AKHS) as I left Kisumu for Nairobi because of AKHS stellar academic reputation. My initial foreboding was overcome as I befriended Firoz Jiwani and entered into a life-long friendship, sharing career paths in Pharmacy to owning pharmacies in Canada. We looked forward to our Friday afternoons of cricket after school and before Jamatkhana with classmates, Mehboob Karmali, Mohamed Jiwa, and the late Alnoor Teja. Little did we know that our friendships and cricket playing camaraderies would sustain our friendships in North America.

Having learnt many lessons from the ironies of life, I accept that destiny has shaped my life. Strange as it may seem but a chance meeting at a convention, braved the opening of a conversation between two strangers providing grounds for business opportunities when our ideas were exchanged. The two strangers are Aziz Dhalla, a fellow pharmacist, from Wales and myself. Aziz and I reconnected in Toronto six months after our chance meeting in England, to enter a business partnership in North Bay, five hours drive from Toronto. North Bay is a quaint town of 50,000, home of the Dionne Quintuplets, and The Gateway to the North. North Bay is located on the traditional territory of the Nipissing First Nation peoples.

We arrived in North Bay on a sunny fall day with a financial guarantee from the Industrial Promotion Services, one of the companies that form part of the Aga Khan Development Network. With their support, we secured a loan from the Scotia Bank to purchase Harris Drugs in1976, on the coldest day of the year, with a temperature of minus 44 Celsius and a wind chill of minus 52 Celsius! Youth, vision and hunger to succeed turned a single pharmacy ownership into two medical centres with 12 medical suites each and a pharmacy which also helped revitalize North Bay's downtown.

Our move to Ottawa in 1994 was prompted due to greater business opportunities and over the years, we acquired numerous pharmacies. My son Karim and I own four IDA drug stores and are presently building a state of the art Drug Preparation Premise at our Richmond medical centre complex for our pharmacy and twelve doctors' offices.

I met Azmina (nee Jadavji), who was a product of Uganda expulsion, at a dinner and dance organized by Ismaili youth in Toronto. Typical of a man in his twentiesy , my aspirations to complete my life with the love of Azmina commenced with our courtship, marriage, and two children, Farah and Karim. I was blessed with a supportive family as I immersed myself to being an entrepreneur, family man and a volunteer for multiple community associations and boards.

My commitment to the three important aspects of my life demanded a work life balance strategy. I did not wish to regret lack of attention or absence from any of my commitments nor did I wish to take for granted that conflicts of work and personal life would automatically work itself. What advice would I offer hard-driving entrepreneurs regarding conflicts? Make time for non-work activities, exercise to reduce stress, learn to say "no," manage your time more efficiently. There are mortgages to be paid, investments to be handled, health to be managed, and children to be raised. There is no magic formula and I hope some guiding principles adopted in my personal life may help. In my experience, successes are due to working extraordinarily hard and it helps, if loved ones are understanding and supportive:

- Give the best you can to your personal life and try to do better. Perfection is not attainable, so expect to fall short some of the time.
- Work and personal life are inextricably intertwined as work supports loved ones; it is a big part of identities and shapes social lives.
- Be present in spirit and body when with family and friends.
- Your body and soul are important so don't forget yourself.

I must confess that the best recollections of inner peace come from humanistic giving and improving lives of the sick and vulnerable. Gratification from volunteer work for charity and benefiting others was time well-spent. During the mid-70s, as founding members of Ismaili Pharmacist Association of Ontario we helped new arrivals with early settlement in Canada. It was quite a remarkable achievement that, of the 70 members, almost 30 were independent pharmacy owners, a testament to the entrepreneurial spirit within the community.

The Association is still in existence and is now part of the alliance under the auspices of the Aga Khan Economic Planning Board of Canada. In 1989, 25 members of the Association donated a Poison Control Centre to Aga Khan University in Karachi. The Specialist in Poison Information can be a registered nurse or pharmacist with specialized training in toxicology. Our association has been grateful for the privilege of this initiative and being able to save lives. The core values of hard work, education, generosity, and service to the community were instilled by our families and AKHS. I enrolled at Shenandoah University for a Doctor of Pharmacy Degree, as one is never too old to further one's education!

Our family life was comfortable in North Bay but after many years there, we recognized the need for religious and cultural grounding through interactions with a larger community, so we moved to Ottawa.

Through a chance happening, we celebrated our 25th anniversary with Firoz and Farah at their home in the eternal city of lights, Paris, exposing us to the true Parisian way of life. Firoz joined Azmina and I to climb Mount Kilimanjaro, an experience which some of my AKHS classmates had undertaken during high school. To call the summit of Mount Kilimanjaro 'The Roof of Africa' hardly does it justice. To me, it was more like the Crown Jewel of Africa and one of the most remarkable experiences of my life. Another memorable holiday was a week-long road trip through the south of France. My lasting bond of friendship with Firoz Jiwani, has stood the test of time based on the rules of trust, honesty, patient listening, respect, loyalty, and being a friend through good and bad times. Our friendship has strengthened with time as we take travel trips, share family kinship, fond memories and future plans.

I have had the good fortune to meet with many special people like our neighbour Jim, who came to my rescue with a baseball bat, ready to pummel the robber who was trying to rob our store of narcotics. That's a real friend, right there, someone who's ready to step up for you through thick and thin. The Beckets, as we affectionately refer to them, continue to be some of our dearest and closest friends.
"Friendship is the hardest in the world to explain. It's not something you learn in school. If you have not learned the meaning of friendship you really have not learnt anything".
Muhammad Ali

Note: Among the numerous awards Esmail has received and some of his appointments are the A.H Robbins Bowl of Hygeia Award for Outstanding Community Service in Pharmacy, as a member of the Board of Governors of Nippising University College, Vice Chairman, Convenor for Aga Khan University on the Canadian National Committee 23 years, Trustee of the Carleton Place and District Memorial Hospital, and as a member on the Board of Governors at Ashbury College.

Reunion
If ~
by Rudyard Kipling

If you can keep your head when all about you
Are losing theirs and blaming it on you;
If you can trust yourself when all men doubt you,
But make allowance for their doubting too;
If you can wait and not be tired by waiting,
Or being lied about, don't deal in lies,
Or being hated don't give way to hating,
And yet don't look too good, nor talk too wise;

If you can dream – and not make dreams your master;
If you can think – and not make thoughts your aim,
If you can meet with Triumph and Disaster
And treat those two impostors just the same;
If you bear to hear the truth you have spoken
Twisted by knaves to make a trap for fools,
Or watch the things you gave your life to, broken,
And stoop and build' em up with worn-out tools;

If you can make one heap of all your winnings
And risk it on one turn of pitch-and-toss,
And lose, and start again at your beginnings
And never breathe a word about your loss;
If you can force your heart and nerve and sinew
To serve your turn long after they are gone,
And so hold on when there is nothing in you
Except the Will which says to them: "Hold on!"

REUNIONS

The adage "A picture is worth a thousand words" has led to an assembly of reunion snapshots to convey our emotions. The only place for enigmatic years is in our memories.

by Tree.card

To Follow your heart, and intuition,
that should be, your number one mission.
Listen to your inner voice,
Live your life, through your choice.
The point is to love, what you are doing,
Your deepest passions; should be pursuing.
Every moment, live excited,
Every morning, be delighted.
Always look forward, to what is ahead,
your thoughts and wisdom, gracefully spread.
Living life to the fullest, is up to you,
Look in the mirror, always be true.

Epilogue

It is easier to revel in pleasantries as memories of success, achievements and happiness generally enjoyed allow us the privilege of idling our retirement to the luxury of travelling, socializing, reading, going to concerts and theatres, watching plays and movies, yoga and fitness classes, personal trainers, gardening and renovating our homes. Whilst these activities keep one busy they do not qualify as legacy and do not leave an indelible mark for the education attained. Arguably, the purpose of education is using knowledge of the natural and our environment to provide focus on social, academic, cultural and intellectual development for the next generation.

Our education has served us for settlement in a new country showering us with high standards of living and comfortable lifestyles but in my humble opinion our work is not done. We are in a relay race and have the personal responsibility to pass the baton onto the next generation. There is a need to define problems and to proactively engage the next generation in solving problems like climate change, a cure for cancer, low-impact energy generation, and development of people regardless of their faith, origin or gender.

What more is there to say? An epilogue may seem superfluous at first, but this might be the most demanding chapter of the book as it is a call to prepare for the future. A major motivation and intention for writing this book has been to encapsulate the fun of our teenage years but also to create awareness, especially for the younger generation. Experience combined with knowledge provides for a powerful message for the younger generation. An anonymous proverb states that we cannot control the wind, but we can direct the sail, seems appropriate.

A few examples of a bulging suitcase of lessons learnt from experiences is being shared:

- Education does not commence or end through schooling, but a lifelong continuum of learning from the moment you are born till death. Mark Twain said "I have never allowed my schooling to get in the way of my education." Learning is the acquisition of knowledge or skills through study, whilst education is the process through which a society passes on the knowledge, values and skills from one generation to another.
- Dexterity in languages in our diverse and pluralistic world is more important than ever. To be a good global citizen fluent in five or more languages can be highly beneficial. English is lingua franca and is spoken in most countries and ability to speak more languages can be advantageous. With Babbel and Rosetta apps, multilingual capability is facilitating ease in ability to learn other languages and French, Spanish and even Chinese will be important to know.
- An important lesson to be emulated through life is remaining disciplined to enjoying life but ensuring a balanced lifestyle. For me, a balanced life means striking a balance between creating time for the things I have to do and like to do for a happy and contented life. This formula ensures growth as an individual and secures mental peace and wellbeing. The Seven Dimensions include Physical, Intellectual, Environmental, Vocational, Social, Emotional and Spiritual health.
- Knowledge must be experienced, and experience must be lived and applied within the current circumstances of life. Our future is dependent

128

upon decisions we and many others make. Positive contributions from the young can ensure a better world for the future.

- Experiential knowledge suggests good things don't happen automatically but come from a committed drive to actively and consciously prepare for a future instead of waiting for good things to happen. Planning for the future can be simple in listing priorities and passions, followed by research and itemization of plans and goals. You are always preparing for the future even if you do not think of the future. What you experience today is based upon what you accomplished or did not accomplish yesterday. And what you will experience tomorrow will be partially built on what you can accomplish today. Your life is built upon the foundation of the past, and you are building the foundation for the future at this moment.

- The most important lesson I've learned in life is to play the long game. Experiences of the past have been lessons used and parents can share these with the younger generation for them to build upon but ultimately personal experiences are the best teacher to help fully understand and develop. Attempts to plan and better prepare for the future compels one to draw upon past experiences, but the future is not an extension of the past and is not predictable. So how does one prepare for the future amidst radical change in societies, cultures, values and priorities with the future not remotely resembling the past? In my humble opinion, I would suggest preparedness through education as a lifelong process, willingness to adapt, think critically, question, work hard and be observant to changes using experiences to help understand how to react in responses.

- Cumulative experiences are only possible through aging and most cultures honour the elder generation for their wisdom. It does not matter how long you live but it's how you live. The African heritage of storytelling from older adults to the young states that "A youth that does not cultivate friendship with the elderly is like a tree without roots." A Chinese proverb states, "An elderly person at home is like a living golden treasure." And Robert Browning wrote: "Grow old along with me! The best is yet to be, the last of life, for which the first was made."

- There is no crystal ball to comfortably predict the future. What will be the new normal after the coronavirus pandemic? Who knows? But world history is rife with examples of great social upheaval, wars, and natural disasters, pandemics, leading to surges in human and social advancement. Past alerts prepare us for possible future responses. Cautious optimism is a good place to pose a question: "Where is the world going and what must I do for it?"

- Lessons to be learnt in a world divided along political, ethnic and religious lines are diversity, pluralism, globalization, alleviation of poverty and democracy, setting the stage for global peace and development. My experience and reflections in life suggest we have not mastered creating a better world through development and have a long way to go as there is a need for genuine concern in initiatives being introduced as fair for all parties.

My thinking is guided by one of the largest development entities in the world, The Aga Khan Development Network, founded by the Aga Khan. This network is a group of institutions that has the manpower and research to offer tangible direction and solutions to impact living conditions and opportunities in the developed and developing world as the world is shrinking and we are interconnected. Integrated mandates ranging from health, education, architecture, culture, micro-finance, disaster mitigation, rural development, promotion of the private sector to revitalization of historic cities, ensures dialogue between the recipient and the planner to ensure effective development models. It is continued dialogue in the design and delivery of programs to yield favourable outcomes.

We are growing older and entering the next stage of our lives, whether that be adulthood, middle age or old age. How well prepared we are for this stage, mentally, physically, financially and spiritually will be determined by how well we have prepared for this stage.

My dear schoolmates, classmates, cohort East Africans, as newcomers to Canada as our home, we have met with varied challenges ranging from lack of Canadian experience, to juggling kids, parents and in-laws in a new country with meagre personal finances. Discipline, courage, strength, hard work and humility helped us surmount settlement hardships to become an integral part of the Canadian fabric. Bravo and cheers to us for the resilience and persistence demonstrated in the early years of settlement. Our journeys have been impressive and with confidence and optimism I look forward to the next generation building on the successes of the foundation and overcoming challenges different from the ones we experienced.

Writing this book has brought back many joyful and tearful memories, and long reflections on where we have come from and what we have achieved as individuals and as a diasporic community. We may not all have been as successful as we would have liked but I believe that few, if any, would rather have chosen any path other than that which destiny planned for us and which we embraced.

It is my fervent hope that those mentioned within these pages, and even those omitted, will recall the days of our youth with fondness, and remember those we have long forgotten. I also hope these anecdotes help those who are younger and born outside Kenya, to better understand the cultural eccentricities of their older family members. Youth in any generation is little different in the emotions and escapades they encounter in making the experience enigmatic upon reflection.

Snapshots

Quadrangle – center of all activities

Quadrangle showing the stairs under which guys sat with mirrors

Quadrangle – center of all activities

Ismaili Jamat khane Nairobi decorated for special celebrations including to honor the Queen's birthday, Independence

History/Economic Club 1969

Prefects 1969

Prom Celebration – Excitement

Cumulative brain power for School Magazine

References:

Mohammed Arkoun, What is Globalization? 2000
Gascoigne, Bamber. HistoryWorld. From 1900-1969,
http://www.historyworld.net
Naipaul, S (1990). India. A million mutinies now London:
William Heinemann Ltd.
https://www.livepopulation.com/country/kenya.html
retrieved March 3, 2020
https://www.familyfriendpoems.com/poems retrieved
March 3, 2020
https://blog.tree.cards/poems retrieved March 3, 2020
https://www.bing.com/images/Aga Khan High School
Nairobi retrieved March 3, 2020
ww.newhttps://wmessage.org/the-message/volume-
3/living-way-knowledge/preparing-for-the-future retrieved
10th July,2020

CPSIA information can be obtained
at www.ICGtesting.com
Printed in the USA
BVHW052203130721
611528BV00002B/14

9 781777 543006